# Here's Another Way to Look At It

## Encouragement
## for the Daily Ups and Downs of Life

*Inspired by Faith*

Here's Another Way to Look At It
©Product Concept Mfg., Inc.

Here's Another Way to Look At It
ISBN 978-0-9914172-3-0
Published by Product Concept Mfg., Inc.
2175 N. Academy Circle #200, Colorado Springs, CO 80909

Written and Compiled by Patricia Mitchell
in association with Product Concept Mfg., Inc.

All scripture quotations are from the King James version
of the Bible unless otherwise noted.

Scriptures taken from the Holy Bible,
New International Version®, NIV®.
Copyright © 1973, 1978, 1984 by Biblica, Inc.™
Used by permission of Zondervan.
All rights reserved worldwide.
www.zondervan.com

Sayings not having a credit listed are contributed by writers
for Product Concept Mfg., Inc. or in a rare case,
the author is unknown.

# Here's Another Way to Look At It

It's not what you look at that matters,
it's what you see.

*Henry David Thoreau*

Have you ever seen something in a whole new way? You're struck by the beauty of a flower, or the splendor of a starry sky—it's an awesome experience! Occasions like these draw you to a deeper appreciation of the world around you.

In a similar way, how you view your cares, concerns, and circumstances changes when you look at them with new eyes. With just a little shift in perspective, you'll be surprised to discover amazing possibilities in ordinary circumstances...valuable opportunities for growth, and insight in adversity... compassion for the viewpoint of another...great potential in the smallest opening in front of you

This is a collection of thoughts designed to offer you another way to look at life—another way to consider your feelings, evaluate your responsibilities, and get the most out of the present moment. Topics ranging from practical to spiritual are treated with a touch of humor and lighthearted fun, all with the help of our outspoken critters. Whether you read each section in order, or pick one that appeals to you, you'll find something good to take with you during the day.

We hope this book brings you uplifting encouragement, inspiration, perhaps something to smile about, and most of all...*another way to look at it!*

I fancy that totally
put-together look,
don't you?

# So many choices…

…*so many things to do!* We can find ourselves wearing so many different hats during the day that we don't quite know who we are or what it is exactly we're trying to accomplish!

If this sounds familiar, why not put on your thinking cap—or better yet, your dreaming cap— for a few minutes? Think about your aspirations. This includes work-related goals, personal goals, where in your life you'd like to be in, say, one, two, or three years. Picture you: your appearance, involvements, interests, and relationships.

Now, how much of what takes up your time today will get you to where you want to find your- self tomorrow? For example, if your goal is more money in the bank next year, do this year's spend- ing and savings patterns support that objective? If you're looking toward a better job or a promotion soon, are you doing something now to build your skills and enhance your résumé? If you're dreaming of a healthier or happier you, what steps are you taking to make that dream a reality?

How many hats are you going to wear, and which ones? You can get it together today for a completely put-together you tomorrow!

*It's another way to look at it!*

# Ever notice…

…how one colorful outfit spices up your wardrobe? It's not far from what happens when you bring a new goal into your life—one you really can get excited about. Energy to do and accomplish brightens your mornings, and your sense of purpose makes you feel good (and look good) all day long.

…how a big project is like a long walk? You'll never succeed with either one if you try to take it in one long stride. But if you go one step at a time—now that's something you can start right now.

…how much fun it is to share your goals with friends? They'll encourage you, and their support will affirm your good ideas. It's possible they'll even have some tips to help you out!

…how time just seems to slip away? It might be hard to say "no" to certain people who ask you to join this group or that committee, but it's the only way to spend your time on things that mean the most to you.

…how happy thoughts are like a sparkly pair of earrings? They make you smile, and when you're smiling, you don't just look good—you look great!

*Ever notice* how good you feel when you have it all together?

*They go together...*

dreams and deeds
ideas and invention
patience and practice
aims and action
risk and reward
work and worth
purpose and pleasure
milestones and making it!

A rock pile ceases to be a rock pile the
moment a single man contemplates it,
bearing within him the image of a cathedral.
*Antoine de Saint-Exupery*

# Plan your work...

Never put off until tomorrow what you can do today, because if you enjoy it today, you can do it again tomorrow.

Happy are those who have a dream and are willing to spend whatever it takes to make it come true.

To make your dream come true, you have to stay awake.

A day is a span of time no one is wealthy enough to waste.

Who begins too much accomplishes nothing.

Aim at nothing, and you're sure to succeed.

Those who do nothing but wait for their ship to come in have already missed the boat.

## ...and work your plan!

# Quotable...

First say to yourself what you would be,
and then do what you have to do.
*Epictetus*

What do you want most to do? That's what I have
to keep asking myself, in the face of difficulties.
*Katherine Mansfield*

Where no plan is laid, where the disposal of time
is surrendered merely to the chance of incident,
chaos will soon reign.
*Victor Hugo*

Our plans miscarry because they have no aim.
When a man does not know what harbor he is
making for, no wind is the right wind.
*Seneca*

Can anything be sadder than work left unfinished?
Yes; work never begun.
*Christina Rossetti*

Far away there in the sunshine are my highest
aspirations. I may not reach them, but I can
look up and see their beauty, believe in them,
and try to follow where they lead.
*Louisa May Alcott*

# MAKING YOUR BREAKS

There's nothing like the feeling
of wind through your mane!

# Some people seem to get all the good breaks…

*…but how good is a good break if you don't recognize it?* How much help is a great opportunity if you're not prepared to take it?

Many excellent life-enhancing openings are available, but they rarely come as bolts out of the blue. Instead, they're created as you build, day by day, your experience and know-how. A reputation for dependability, honesty, adaptability, and good character sets you high above the rest, and gets you noticed. And when you're noticed by opportunity (in the guise of teachers and mentors, leaders and employers, friends and associates), opportunity comes to you.

Yet that's only half the story. The other half involves your taking it. Though the opportunity offered may not qualify as a big break, it could be the first or second or third step toward it. It's your chance to show your adaptability, flexibility, and willingness to try. Then again, the opportunity might look so big that it scares you silly! Take it anyway.

While it may seem as if some people get all the breaks every time, reality is more like this: They're constantly learning and growing, exploring and discovering, stepping (and sometimes leaping) when chances come their way. They're living every day with their eyes open wide and their feet moving forward!

*It's another way to look at it!*

# Opportunity knocks,
# but some people…

… don't hear it because they're sound asleep.

… don't want it because they're comfortable
where they are.

… won't let it in because it's disguised as a problem.

… don't see it because they're out looking for a
four-leafed clover.

… can't entertain it because they're afraid to
invite it in.

… don't recognize it because it's not labeled
OPPORTUNITY.

… let it get away while they're wondering whether
they want to take it.

*Opportunity knocks—*
*are you going to open the door?*

# Quotable…

Opportunity is missed by most people because it is dressed in overalls and looks like work.
*Thomas Alva Edison*

You had better live your best and act your best and think your best today; for today is the sure preparation for tomorrow and all the other tomorrows that follow.
*Harriet Martineau*

The world is all gates, all opportunities, strings of tension waiting to be struck.
*Ralph Waldo Emerson*

To face every opportunity of life thoughtfully, and ask its meaning bravely and earnestly, is the only way to meet the supreme opportunities when they come, whether open-faced or disguised.
*Maltbie Davenport Babcock*

To succeed, jump as quickly at opportunities as you do at conclusions.
*Benjamin Franklin*

In great affairs we ought to apply ourselves less to creating chances than to profiting from those that are offered.
*François de La Rochefoucauld*

# Attention! Caution! Action!

*Attention!*

Big breaks rarely present themselves, but count-less small ones regularly do. You're more likely, for instance, to build a sizable savings account by saving a little each month than by relying on a fortune to come your way. You're more assured of better health by exercising today than by waiting for a mir-acle drug. You're more equipped for excellence by working steadily than by holding off until a spectac-ular opening comes your way.

*Caution!*

Not every opportunity that comes, however, is right for you. An opportunity may promise fame, status, travel, and wealth, but it could mean doing things guaranteed to bring trouble into your life. You might get what it promises (or not), but along with a tarnished reputation, an unsettled con-science, and lowered self-esteem.

Exercise caution, too, if you're offered fabulous opportunities that answer your dearest dreams and then some. If you haven't entered the contest, you didn't win it. If you don't have the background, training, or expertise, ask why have you been select-ed. As the adage says, "If it's too good to be true, it probably is."

*Action!*

Opportunity after opportunity could open for you, but not one benefits you unless you reach out and take it. And then run with it! Your true "big break" is the one that builds on the skills and talents you already have, and challenges you to reach the next level of accomplishment. It strengthens your confidence, preparing you for the next "big break" that comes your way.

While you're taking action, remember that many people around you are taking action, too. They're the teachers and mentors who give you direction, advice and guidance...friends who encourage you, boost your spirits, and celebrate your milestones with you...coworkers, peers, and associates who are working right alongside you. They help you succeed. They open doors for you, and you need to open doors for them. One good turn deserves another, which generates further opportunity for you.

Take action! Before you know it, the "big break"—the one you've been dreaming of—is right in front of you. You've worked for it, you've earned it, and you're ready to take it on!

# God gives us the nuts…

Those that are afraid of bad opportunities will never know good ones.

Happy chances and fortunate coincidences are most often with those who don't include them in their plans.

The sign on the door of opportunity often reads "Push."

Golden opportunities are not found at the end of a rainbow.

Combine common sense and the Golden Rule, and you will see very little misfortune cross your path.

Good fortune is good planning, well executed.

## …but He doesn't crack them open for us!

# EAGER TO LEARN

Who says you can't teach
an old dog new tricks?

# It's not the same as when you were a mere pup…

*…things have changed,* and they keep changing. Though every generation—every individual—has obstacles of some kind to overcome, today we're all facing a number of challenges.

Our awareness of world events is unprecedented, yet the information often brings concerns about our peace and security. Employers' needs for flexibility in their business plans means that heightened worker training and adaptability is vital. The ideal family has been redefined by many, leading to a renewed emphasis on nourishing and maintaining relationships.

If you feel as if you're jumping through hoops at every turn, you're right!

Yet you can make things work for you. Daily news about places across the globe invites you to explore cultures other than your own. Lifelong education increases your know-how and keeps your mind sharp. Your relationships, no longer taken for granted, prompt you to cherish those you love every day.

Through it all, however, there's one constant: God doesn't change. He's there for you, just as He was for all generations past, no matter how many hoops you have dangling in front of you today!

*It's another way to look at it!*

# If "old dogs" can't learn new tricks, then how come…

… so many parents and grandparents embrace and use technology that they could never have conceived of in their younger years?

… so many men and women are on their second or third careers, each one more fulfilling than the last?

… so many students and young adults have the freedom to explore a vast array of opportunities, maybe even switch their life's direction in an entirely new direction?

… so many children, far from having their occupation handed down to them, see a world of possibilities open to them?

… the happiest people are those who continue to grow, discover, and bloom with each new stage in life?

*"Old dog," "young pup," or somewhere in between,* you can meet the challenge of not only living in, but thriving in, these heady, exhilarating times!

# Quotable…

We attempt nothing great but from the sense of the difficulties we have to encounter; we persevere in nothing great but from a pride in overcoming them.
*William Hazlitt*

If I had a formula for bypassing trouble, I would not pass it round. Trouble creates a capacity to handle it. I don't embrace trouble; that's as bad as treating it as an enemy. But I do say meet it as a friend, for you'll see a lot of it and had better be on speaking terms with it.
*Oliver Wendell Holmes*

It is not in the still calm of life, or in the repose of a pacific station, that great characters are formed… the habits of a vigorous mind are formed contending with difficulties. All history will convince you of this, and that wisdom and penetration are the fruit of experience, not the lessons of retirement and leisure. Great necessities call out great virtues.
*Abigail Adams*

If an obstacle is put in our path, it is only to prevent us from going the wrong way, and to guide us into what is for us the only right path.
*Henry Thomas Hamblin*

*Vision is the art of seeing things invisible.*
Jonathan Swift

*Embrace* a better path…bigger world…broader experience…higher purpose…deeper relationships…greater expectations…fuller satisfaction…believe in *all your possibilities.*


*Everyone who got where he is*
*had to begin where he was.*
Robert Louis Stevenson

*Learn* how to throw a basketball…create a quilt…paint a landscape…swim a mile…decorate a room…climb a mountain…hike a trail…make a sandcastle…build a snowman…plant a garden…do something you've always put off until "later."


*We must believe that we are gifted for something,*
*and that this thing, at whatever cost,*
*must be attained.*
Marie Curie

*Discover* inner strengths you never knew you possessed…natural talents that have never had a chance to develop…what it's like to follow your own heart, celebrate your own dreams…self-confidence that comes only from knowing you can do it, *because you have.*

# If you want a place in the sun...

A bend in the road is not the end of the road—
unless you fail to make the turn.

Smooth seas do not make skillful sailors.

Turn your stumbling blocks into stepping stones.

Hope is the anchor of the soul, the stimulus to
action, and the incentive to achievement.

God gave us burdens, but also shoulders.

The difficulties of life are intended to make us
better, not bitter.

Things turn out best for those who make the
best of the way things turn out.

## ...you've got to expect a few blisters.

# AVOIDING THE POTHOLES

Please don't step on my roof!

# You can't avoid them all…

*…but you sure can swerve around a lot of them,* and you can generally see them ahead of you. Life's potholes are nothing less than places others have stumbled into so often that there are proverbs posted as warning signs: Waste not, want not. Better late than never. Idle hands are the devil's workshop. Look before you leap. All things come to those who wait.

You'd think "a word to the wise would be sufficient," but there are times when nothing less than a trip, or a full-blown fall, into a wide-open pothole will do. Overspend, the bills pile up, and it's no surprise to stumble into debt. Rush an important decision, and stub your toe on a poor choice. Act impulsively, and a less than happy consequence is hardly unexpected.

While it's best to heed the warnings, a stepped-in pothole is an effective teacher. Now you know what it feels like, so the level of your empathy for others in a similar situation rises dramatically. You realize mistakes can happen to anyone, even those who "know better." Also, you find out first-hand how to dig yourself out, dust yourself off, and keep going forward, because the only thing worse than falling into a pothole is staying there.

*It's another way to look at it!*

# Proverbial wisdom revisited...

An early bird catches the worm...
but the early worm is the one that gets caught.

If you can't stand the heat...
run through a sprinkler.

A penny saved is...
not much anymore.

Laugh and the world laughs with you; cry and you...
have to blow your nose.

Strike while the...
bug is not moving.

Look before you...
drive over the curb.

Where there's smoke...
there's pollution.

A miss is as good as a...
mister.

It's always darkest before...
Daylight Savings Time.

An idle mind is the...
best way to relax.

# HEADLINE?

*Time-honored truths* are like fences that stop you from straying onto dangerous paths...curbs that prevent you from doing or saying that one thing that unravels relationships...stepping stones that guide you when you're not sure where to go.

If you ignore them, thinking such ancient thoughts could have no relevance to this modern age, you discover another time-honored truth: that though the world may change, people don't. Envy, selfishness, gossip, and pride still wreak havoc; contentment, generosity, kindness, and humility still create a happy, meaningful life.

Though labeled as obsolete, time-honored truths outlast trends, fads, and new philosophies. Though a few dismiss them, time-honored truths are at home with millions who quietly go about their day with dignity, integrity, and love for others. Though called old-fashioned by some, time-honored truths still wear well—very, very well—for all.

# Quotable…

Nobody can acquire honor by doing what is wrong.
*Thomas Jefferson*

You cannot do wrong without suffering wrong.
*Ralph Waldo Emerson*

Don't ever take a fence down until you know the
reason why it was put up.
*G. K. Chesterton*

Care for the truth more than what people think.
*Aristotle*

Of all the paths a man could strike into, there is,
at any given moment, a best path…a thing which,
here and now, it were of all things wisest for him
to do…to find this path, and walk in it, is the one
thing needful for him.
*Thomas Carlyle*

Expedients are for the hour; principles for the ages.
*Henry Ward Beecher*

True wisdom consists in not departing from nature
and in molding our conduct according to her laws.
*Seneca*

We are less likely to fail if we measure with judgment our chances and our capabilities.
*Agnes Repplier*

There is in the worst of fortune the best of chances for a happy change.
*Euripides*

The voice of conscience is so delicate that it is easy to stifle it; but it is also so clear that it is impossible to mistake it.
*Madame de Staël*

Learn to see in another's calamity the ills which you should avoid.
*Publilius Syrus*

Forget the times of your distress, but never forget what they taught you.
*Herbert Spencer Gasser*

Whenever you fall, pick something up.
*Oswald Avery*

# HEALING THE HURTS

Forgive me?

# When you hurt…

*…you hurt.* Your friends try to comfort you with well-meant words of encouragement, and you appreciate their concern. They urge you to let it go, and you nod in agreement. You know they're right, but you just can't manage to forget the pain you felt when you were deceived…criticized…left alone. It changed everything.

What are you going to do? Sure, you could take revenge, but you know that would put you on the level of the person who hurt you. Or you could start viewing your relationships through the lens of bitterness and cynicism. Or you could choose to forgive, truly forgive from your heart.

Only forgiveness is capable of healing your hurt. No, you're not going to forget what happened, because it's a paragraph, or possibly a chapter, of your life's story. But it isn't the whole story. You have joys to remember, successes to celebrate, relationships to savor, and hope to lift your eyes toward tomorrow.

Even if it's not possible to personally offer your offender forgiveness, or the person refuses it, forgive for your own sake. Forgiveness alone has the power to provide the peace you're yearning for—and the peace you need. Will you let this offender continue to hurt you? Are you going to let the wound remain open forever?

*It's another way to look at it!*

# *Forgiveness* frees you from...

... living with hostility and anger, self-pity and bitterness, resentment and cynicism.

...carrying the burden of hatred and living with the guilt of a grudge.

... bearing the weight of anxiety and depression.

... allowing someone else, a situation, or your own memories to determine your life.

... focusing exclusively on an unfortunate, negative, or traumatic event.

... letting volatile emotions continue to determine how you view what happened.

... needing to justify yourself whenever the incident comes to mind or you talk about it with others.

# *Forgiveness* frees you to…

… take control of yourself, your life, your story,
   and your perspective.

… enjoy wholesome, life-enhancing relationships
   with others now and in the future.

… give thanks for the wonderful parts of your life
   and for the blessings you enjoy.

… concentrate on the good that has happened in
   the past and the good you can look forward to
   in the future.

… empathize with the hurts of others, and maybe
   begin to understand the suffering of your offender.

… move peacefully from yesterday to today…
   from today into tomorrow.

# Forgive? Yes!

# *Forgiveness* is not for the forgiven…

Forgiveness does not originate from a position of weakness, but is a consequence of strength.

Only the brave know how to forgive.

Bitterness causes pain and lethargy. It is when we learn how to let go that new possibilities appear.

Keep doing what you're doing, and you'll keep getting what you're getting.

To be wronged is nothing unless you continue to remember it.

*To forgive is to set yourself free.*

# …but for the sake of the forgiver.

# Quotable...

Everyone says forgiveness is a lovely idea
until they have something to forgive.
*C. S. Lewis*

Forgiveness saves the expense of anger,
the cost of hatred.
*Hannah More*

Forgiveness is the fragrance the violet sheds
on the heel that has crushed it.
*Mark Twain*

If ye forgive men their trespasses,
your heavenly Father will also forgive you.
*Matthew 6:14*

It is easier to forgive an enemy than to
forgive a friend.
*William Blake*

Always forgive your enemies—
nothing annoys them so much.
*Oscar Wilde*

# Stepping stones to true forgiveness…

…find the good in it, no matter how difficult the situation. You're wiser now; you're stronger because you've come through difficulties that might have destroyed a weaker person; you realize how fragile life is, so you're kinder, gentler, and more sympathetic than you were before.

…separate your emotions from what happened, and reflect objectively on the events. Try to put yourself in the other's shoes and imagine what might have been going through his or her mind—not to excuse, but to understand human frailties and mistakes; acknowledge mental and emotional limitations that may have played a significant part.

…realize that you're never going to be free, but remain a victim, unless you forgive. There's no other way! Whether the person ever admits wrongdoing, offers a meaningful apology, or accepts your forgiveness matters little. What matters is that forgiveness benefits you. It brings you peace. It heals wounds. It works.

# PRESSING ON

Are we there yet?

# Is it all worth it?

*Most of us have asked that question at some point.* We're in a slow-as-a-turtle line at the airport, and at the last minute our flight is canceled. Frustrated, we wonder, "Is it all worth it?" But once we've arrived at our destination and we're sitting down at the dinner table with family and friends, we sigh with contentment. Yes, it was worth the aggravation to be at this place, at this time.

During long and sometimes difficult journeys—child-raising, caregiving, career-building, goal-reaching—the question, "Is it worth it?" comes to mind. When it does, take a few moments to remember why you're on this journey in the first place. You want to give your best to your children, your loved ones...you desire experience and expertise in your work...you hope to achieve a meaningful goal.

The reason why of your journey far outweighs the day-to-day hassles, troubles, and frustrations you experience. If you give it up now, it's like turning around mid-air, going back home, and shutting the door behind you. Yes, you would avoid some temporary discomfort, but you would miss the journey and the joys, experiences, wisdom, and rewards that make for a fulfilling and satisfying life.

Keep going, because the journey—and the destination—are worth the best you have to give.

*It's another way to look at it!*

# A little lift of laughter...

*Asking...Asking...*

A passenger on a cruise ship was standing on deck when he spotted a bearded, ragged-looking man waving frantically from a dot of an island in the ocean. Immediately the passenger alerted the captain, took him out to the deck, and pointed to the man, more and more distant as the ship moved on. "Oh yes," the captain said, "but that's normal. Every time we pass this point, he gets out there and does that."

*Just a Question*

One afternoon a proud new mom was walking with her infant daughter in the stroller. When she saw a woman approaching them with her little poodle on a leash, Mom bent down to her daughter and exclaimed, "See the pretty doggy?" But she quickly straightened up as she realized the woman may have heard her asking an infant a question as if she expected an answer. Just then, as the woman passed, she leaned over to her poodle and said, "See the little baby?"

*Practical Answer*

A driver, going well over the speed limit, was pulled over by a state trooper. As he was handing over his license, the driver asked, "How come I'm the one who was stopped when everyone else was speeding, too?"

The trooper glanced in the back seat and noticed fishing gear. "I see you're a fisherman," he said.

"Yes, officer, I am," said the man, puzzled at the comment.

"So, have you ever caught *all* the fish you're looking at?"

*...to help along the way!*

# You're not there yet…

Perseverance is the ability to follow through on an idea long after the mood has passed.

Success is measured by the willingness to keep trying.

The race is not always to the swift, but to those who keep on running.

Don't be discouraged. It's often the last key in the bunch that opens the lock.

We rate ability in people by what they finish, not by what they begin.

Don't leave before the miracle happens!

Those who cannot endure the bad will never make it to see the good.

## …but you're closer than you were yesterday!

# Quotable...

When you get into a tight place and everything
goes against you, till it seems as though you could
not hang on a minute longer, never give up then, for
that is just the place and time that the tide will turn.
*Harriet Beecher Stowe*

That which we persist in doing becomes easier—
not that the nature of the task has changed,
but our ability to do it has increased.
*Ralph Waldo Emerson*

Endure and persist; this pain will turn to
good by and by.
*Ovid*

Learn to self-conquest, persevere thus for a time,
and you will perceive very clearly the advantage
which you gain from it.
*Teresa of Avila*

Be like a postage stamp—stick to one thing until
you get there.
*Josh Billings*

# TAKING A LEAP

## Who says I can't fly?

# Living is risky…

*…because daily decisions, actions, and choices* don't come with guarantees, and never have. If you choose, for instance, to try something new or go forward in a fresh direction, there's a risk things won't turn out the way you had anticipated. But then again, there's a good chance you'll discover all you had hoped, and then some.

Take no risks? That's a risk in itself! You limit your maturity, development, and experience, because growth takes place every time you dare to venture beyond the boundaries of your present circumstances. You open yourself to later regrets of "what could have been" if you never explore opportunities that interest you now. By never taking a leap into the unknown, you're almost assured of a mundane, lackluster existence. Win or lose, succeed or fail, or end up somewhere in between, you have seen, learned, experienced, and discovered more about yourself and the world.

There's a difference, however, between smart and not-so-smart risks. Shows of derring-do, life-threatening tricks, and rash decisions are definitely far from smart. But with adequate thinking and planning, along with advice from people whose experience and wisdom you trust, the intelligent, calculated risks you choose to take will work to your ultimate good.

*It's another way to look at it!*

*All life is risk!* Whatever you do (or don't do), you risk the disapproval of others, even those closest to you. By keeping the status quo, you risk never reaching your potential. By branching out, you risk stumbling, even falling. But even if you do, you have the satisfaction of having tried.

*Examine the risk,* because leaping without looking puts you in avoidable danger. Get as much information as you can, and weigh what mature, experienced people tell you. Intelligent risks can withstand the harsh light of time and scrutiny.

*Listen to yourself.* If your conscience says "no," don't do it. If a voice deep inside you whispers that this really isn't what you want, back off, even if your best friends tell you it's a wonderful opportunity. If a gut feeling warns you, take heed!

*Put the level of risk into perspective.* With any life-altering decision or significant change, there are pros and cons. Weigh them objectively, separating fantasy fears from realistic possibilities. Hear what others tell you, because they are seeing from another point of view.

*Take calculated risks.* An impulsive decision is just that—an impulsive decision. While it may work out okay, or even yield great rewards, another risk presents itself. Those who believe they have the magical power to win by making snap decisions sooner or later find out otherwise.

*Make your decision,* and then go for it. Don't lose your focus by looking back; even if your decision proves wrong, you cannot undo what you have done. It's better to admit that you made a mistake than to remain in a bad situation out of stubbornness or false pride. See what options are available to you now.

*Embrace risk!* Risk provides adventure, excitement, discovery, and fulfillment. It's the only way to explore your possibilities, reach your potential, and live your dreams.

# Quotable…

Prudence keeps life safe, but does not often make it happy.
*Samuel Johnson*

The soul should always stand ajar, ready to welcome the ecstatic experience.
*Emily Dickinson*

For of all sad words of tongue or pen, the saddest are these: It might have been.
*John Greenleaf Whittier*

Do the hardest thing on earth for you. Act for yourself. Face the truth.
*Katherine Mansfield*

No one reaches a high position without daring.
*Publilius Syrus*

Without risk, faith is an impossibility.
*Søren Kierkegaard*

The fishermen know that the sea is dangerous and the storm terrible, but they have never found these dangers sufficient reason for remaining ashore.
*Vincent van Gogh*

# Take risks! If you win,
# you will be happy…

Nothing ventured, nothing gained.

If the risk-reward ratio is right,
you can make big money buying trouble.

Security is not the absence of risk,
but the presence of God, no matter what the risk.

Those who forecast all perils will never sail the sea.

More noble than the will to win is the courage
to begin.

Danger and delight grow on one stalk.

# …if you lose,
# you will be wise.

# ASKING QUESTIONS

Curiosity did *what* to the cat??

# "Why?"...

*...is a question* we asked a dozen times a day when we were kids. Growing older, however, we tend to forget about "why?" and simply accept things the way they are. For sure, some things are beyond our ability to fully grasp, like the awesome love of God for each one of us. "That's just the way it is" remains the only response to many spiritual mysteries.

But how about other things? Asking "why?" can lead you to a deeper knowledge of events and circumstances that affect you. You may not be able to change them—or you may choose not to—yet "why" will help you bear with them and feel you have some mastery over them. "Why?" might prompt better methods of managing hardship or adversity, and work to clarify or redirect your thinking, actions, and emotions. "Why?" in relationships opens conversation, builds support, and increases understanding of others and yourself.

"Why?" doesn't only bring insight, self-awareness, and a sense of control—there's an added benefit. The "why?" that moved you to investigate further, uncover more, and dig until you came up with the facts is the "why?" that makes you a helpful friend and interesting conversationalist, too!

*It's another way to look at it!*

# Quotable...

The habits of a vigorous mind are formed in contending with difficulties.
*Abigail Adams*

Curiosity is lying in wait for every secret.
*Ralph Waldo Emerson*

I am never afraid of what I know.
*Anna Sewell*

Everything that is new or uncommon raises a pleasure in the imagination, because it fills the soul with an agreeable surprise, gratifies its curiosity, and gives it an idea of which it was not before possessed.
*Joseph Addison*

Life must be lived and curiosity kept alive. One must never, for whatever reason, turn his back on life.
*Eleanor Roosevelt*

Curiosity is one of the most permanent and certain characteristics of a vigorous intellect.
*Samuel Johnson*

Be less curious about people and more curious about ideas.
*Marie Curie*

# Let curiosity...

... *open possibilities* by welcoming surprise and serendipity into your life. Embrace unexpected change, different scenery, unfamiliar faces, and a shake-up in your day-to-day routine.

... *invite new ways of thinking.* Listen to or read commentary by speakers who don't reflect your point of view. Reflect on what they're saying, and offer thoughtful responses.

... *re-introduce you to people.* Ask friends—especially those you believe you know well—about their joys and aspirations, their challenges and hopes. Listen respectfully and well.

... *expand your boundaries.* Take a class in a subject you know little or nothing about, yet have an interest in. Learn a skill—painting, weaving, woodworking—that sounds fun to you.

... *accompany tension.* Nervousness when exploring outside your comfort zone is natural. Rather than let tension slow you down, allow it to push you forward into discovery, answers, and satisfaction.

... *color your life.* Following the same routine day after day, year after year, dulls the mind and diminishes happiness. Deliberately go out of your way to meet new people, reflect on diverse ideas, and participate in different activities.

# If you want to know your past, ask your present conditions…

Some people go through a forest and see no firewood.

It's better to ask a question than to remain ignorant.

God hides things by putting them all around us.

Only the curious have something to find.

Those who ask a question are fools for the moment; those who never ask remain fools forever.

Those who resist asking questions never understand answers.

## …if you want to know your future, ask your present actions.

The *path* not taken leads to the *place* never seen.

The *gift* left unopened contains a *treasure*
never possessed.

The *idea* not entertained provides *discernment*
never acquired.

The *voice* not listened to belongs to *understanding*
never developed.

The *wonder* ignored remains *awe* never felt.

The *time* wasted presents *opportunities* never seized.

The *dream* turned away means *fulfillment*
never realized.

The *love* refused is *joy* never experienced.

The *question* not asked stays an *answer* forever
left unknown.

# KNOWING YOURSELF

Hi! I don't believe we've met.

# Imagine, after knowing someone for years...

*...you discover that you really don't know her at all.* It turns out she harbored secrets she never shared, interests she never pursued, potential she never developed, and thoughts she never bothered to speak aloud. Instead of a friend, a stranger stands in front of you.

If this happened, you might feel baffled, or even betrayed. Now imagine how you would feel if that friend you didn't really know is you. After a lifetime of living, you realize there are secrets you have never admitted to yourself, interests you've never tapped, potential you've never tried to reach, and thoughts you've never examined for validity, fairness, or truthfulness.

It's unlikely that you're a complete stranger to yourself, yet most of us keep a portion of ourselves hidden from our true selves. There are things about our past or personality that we'd just as soon not come to grips with. There are traits obvious to others that we refuse to see within ourselves.

Self-improvement, maturity, and spiritual wholeness happen only by going to those places deep inside that have been kept closed for so long. How can change take place if we don't admit what needs changing? How can we offer genuine forgiveness, kindness, love, and respect to others if we withhold it from ourselves?

Imagine knowing—and loving—yourself.

*It's another way to look at it!*

# Do you know…

*…how to ask yourself questions and listen for your answer?* Be a kindly, compassionate friend to you, giving yourself time to express your inmost thoughts. Press gently for deeper answers than the ones you've always told yourself. Ask for more clarity, specificity, and honesty.

*…how to answer for yourself?* Only you know how you truly feel and what you honestly think, not the voice of "should" that shouts so loudly within you, or the opinion of strong-willed and dominant people in your life.

*…how to balance strengths and weaknesses?* Everyone possesses both, but some highlight strengths while ignoring weaknesses; others maximize weaknesses and minimize strengths. Neither way leads you to a balanced knowledge of yourself.

*…how to take responsibility for who you are?* Others have affected your life in significant ways, sometimes even leaving scars and wounds on heart and soul. It takes courage and determination to shun blame and take responsibility for being the kind of person you are and want to be.

*…how to welcome joy into your life?* You cannot find genuine joy if there are unacknowledged fears, unanswered questions, and an undervalued you hidden in the shadows of your heart. Discover yourself, and discover the joy of knowing you.

# Getting to know you…

Many self-discoverers find it useful to keep a record of what they're feeling, thinking, and experiencing. Whether you use a paper journal or online program, putting words where you can see and reread them prompts valuable insight.

It's possible you're always on the go, but you realize your happiest evenings are the ones you spend at home with a good book. Then you might ask yourself why you're out more often than not—are you trying to please or impress others? If so, why? If the opposite is true—you thrive in a group but you rarely go out, why? What's holding you back from participating in new activities and meeting new people?

You can be as brief or as thorough as you want. The most important point is honesty. Your words are between you and yourself, meant to reveal inconsistencies that are keeping you from knowing yourself and honoring yourself by being yourself.

# Quotable…

A humble knowledge of oneself is a surer road
to God than a deep searching of the sciences.
*Thomas à Kempis*

It is not only the most difficult thing to know one's self,
but the most inconvenient.
*Josh Billings*

Not until we are lost do we begin to understand
ourselves.
*Henry David Thoreau*

To know what you prefer, instead of humbly saying
"Amen" to what the world tells you you ought to prefer,
is to keep your soul alive.
*Robert Louis Stevenson*

It is not easy to find happiness in ourselves,
and it is not possible to find it elsewhere.
*Agnes Repplier*

Learn what you are, and be such.
*Pindar*

By all means use sometimes to be alone.
Salute thyself; see what thy soul doth wear.
*George Herbert*

# Every one of us has within a continent of undiscovered character…

We strenuously avoid the questions that will bring us face to face with ourselves.

If you won't allow yourself to get lost, there's a chance you may never be found.

We learn to love ourselves and others not by seeing a perfect person, but by learning to see an imperfect person perfectly.

One stands in his own shadow and wonders why it's dark.

The hardest journey is the one that takes you into your own self.

What we criticize about others is often what we excuse within ourselves.

# …and blessed is he who acts the Columbus to his own soul.

# DISCOVERING PURPOSE

There's nothing like a
nice purposeful nap.

# A sense of purpose gives meaning to life…

*…without it, we're prey to every wind that comes along.* Who knows which way to go when there's no particular destination in mind to begin with?

From an early age, some of us know exactly what we want to do. For others, however, only time and experience reveal our niche, and when we have found it, life takes on a whole new dimension and meaning.

How would you describe your life's purpose? What gives you a sense of oneness with the world and satisfaction in being who you are, where you are? Or do you feel adrift right now, unsure, perhaps, of your purpose anymore? Sometimes circumstances demand a reevaluation of life's purpose, or what had been a strong sense of purpose in the past no longer motivates now. At any stage, you can revitalize the purpose you've had all along, or carefully consider what different course may be open to you.

There's neither magic nor mystery in determining life's purpose. It emerges through clear thinking, an objective look at talents and abilities, and an assessment of responsibilities at hand and the needs around you. The reward of a meaningful, fulfilled life, however, is found in faithfully doing whatever it demands and closely following wherever it leads.

*It's another way to look at it!*

# Quotable...

Have a purpose in life, and having it, throw into your work such strength of mind and muscle as God has given you.
*Thomas Carlyle*

There is no chance, no destiny, no fate that can circumvent or hinder or control the firm resolve of a determined soul.
*Ella Wheeler Wilcox*

A life without purpose is a languid, drifting thing. Every day we ought to review our purpose, saying to ourselves: this day let us make a sound beginning, for what we have hitherto done is naught.
*Thomas à Kempis*

Great minds have purposes; others have wishes.
*Washington Irving*

Seek out that particular mental attribute which makes you feel most deeply and vitally alive, along with which comes the inner voice which says, "This is the real me," and when you have found that attitude, follow it.
*William James*

As soon as you trust yourself, you will know how to live.
*Johann von Goethe*

*One ship sails East,*
*And another West,*
*By the self-same winds that blow—*
*'Tis the set of the sails*
*And not the gales,*
*That tells the way to go.*

*Like the winds of the sea*
*Are the waves of time*
*As we journey along through life—*
*'Tis the set of the soul*
*That determines the goal,*
*And not the calm or the strife.*

Ella Wheeler Wilcox

# A little lift of laughter…

*Today's Purpose: Same as Yesterday*

One morning, Mom walked through the living room and noticed her son lounging on the couch. "What are you planning to do today?" she asked.

"Nothing," he replied.

Irritated, she snapped back, "That's what you told me yesterday!"

"Well," he said, "I'm not done yet."

*Purpose of Prayer?*

Little Kyle and his family were having Sunday dinner at Grandma's house. As soon as everyone was seated around the table and the food served, Kyle picked up his fork and began to eat.

"Kyle!" admonished his mother. "We haven't said our prayer yet."

"We don't need to," the boy replied.

"Of course we do, Kyle," said Mom, "just like we do at home."

"That's at our house," Kyle explained, "but this is Grandma's house, and she knows how to cook!"

*Here for a Purpose*

A young entrepreneur rented his first office space and furnished it lavishly. Sitting behind his impressive-looking desk, he noticed a man enter the outer office. Hoping to appear important, the entrepreneur picked up the phone and began a pretend conversation with a major client. When he finally hung up, he greeted his visitor by asking, "May I help you?"

"Sure," the man replied. "I'm here to hook up your phone."

# Living on Purpose

The great and glorious masterpiece of man is to know
how to live to purpose.
*Michel Montaigne*

To be what we are, and to become what we are capable
of becoming, is the only end of life.
*Robert Louis Stevenson*

Without a purpose, nothing should be done.
*Marcus Aurelius*

The purpose of life seems to be to acquaint a man
with himself.
*Ralph Waldo Emerson*

Laboring toward distant aims sets the mind in a higher
key, and puts us at our best.
*Charles Henry Parkhurst*

Only he who keeps his eye fixed on the far horizon will
find his right road.
*Dag Hammarskjöld*

# BOUNCING BACK

What goes down, must come up,
and I can prove it!

# Jump up in the air...

*...and sometimes we come down with a thud!* Setbacks serve to jolt us out of complacency, and they're often the catalyst for real and significant change. After all, what better than a complete reversal to convince us that the way we're putting things together isn't working for us?

If you're sitting flat on the ground with your life in pieces around you, you're in a perfect position to reassess your plans, principles, needs, and desires. Identify when things started to go down and figure out what you could have done better. You might want to discard habits that have contributed to this most recent setback; eliminate ways of thinking that repeatedly hold you back; adopt standards that motivate you to aim higher and work better; commit yourself to worthwhile, meaningful objectives.

Once you have your feet on the ground, you're ready to start jumping up again. Perhaps you've kept your former goal, but you're going about it differently this time. You've learned some lessons and you've gained helpful experience. Or you've ditched the old plans entirely, and now you have a new idea that reflects a wiser, more mature, you. Either way, you won't get the same outcome, because you're jumping with stronger legs under you this time!

*It's another way to look at it!*

# Good judgment comes from experience…

Challenges make you discover things about yourself that you never really knew. They're what makes the mind stretch—what makes you go beyond the norm.

A happy life isn't so much about how fast you run, or how high you climb, but all about how well you bounce.

Breakdowns can be the beginning of breakthroughs.

For every challenge encountered, there's an opportunity for growth.

Sometimes we have to be torn down before we can be built up.

Adversity comes with instruction in its hand.

We cannot appreciate success unless we've known its lack.

# …and experience comes from poor judgment.

# Remember…

*Even the soundest,* most sensible, and well-thought-out plans can go awry. Unforeseen circumstances can undermine a key provision, or an unlikely occurrence can render prior calculations unusable. Far worse than any setback, however, is letting it keep you back.

*Even if your words or actions played a role* in what happened, you have a chance now to make a fresh start, having learned, matured, and grown through the difficult experience. Offer meaningful apologies where appropriate, repair what damage you can, and then go forward.

*Even if it's a life-altering event,* make the best of it. Know what you can and can't control, and don't waste your energy fighting or denying a new reality. Instead, find a way to minimize its effect on you, or better yet, work in your favor.

*Even if it completely blind-sided you,* refuse to lose heart. Yes, you may need some time to fully comprehend what happened, seek the comfort and counsel of trusted friends and family members, and rest your body and mind. Let those things restore your courage to go on.

*Even if it's not funny in the least,* find a trace of humor in it. Humor will lighten your heart, keep you from over-dramatizing the event (or yourself), broaden your understanding, and provide you with the refreshment you need during a trying time.

# Quotable…

The credit belongs to the man who is actually in the arena, whose face is marred by dust and sweat and blood; who strives valiantly; who errs, who comes short again and again...who knows great enthusiasms, the great devotions; who spends himself in a worthy cause; who at the best, knows in the end the triumph of high achievement; and who, at the worst, if he fails, at least fails while daring greatly, so that his place shall never be with those cold and timid souls who neither know victory nor defeat.
*Theodore Roosevelt*

Within us there are wells of thought and dynamos of energy which are not suspected until emergencies arise. Then oftentimes we find that it is comparatively simple to double or triple our former capacities and to amaze ourselves by the results achieved.
*Thomas J. Watson*

*Oh, a trouble's a ton,*
*or a trouble's an ounce,*
*Or a trouble is what you make it,*
*And it isn't the fact*
*that you're hurt than counts,*
*But only how you take it.*
Edmund Vance Cooke

# DRAWING THE LINES

So like I said, you've got to draw
the lines somewhere!

# We hear a lot about healthy personal boundaries…

*…and how we need to draw them* when people take advantage of our time, invade our privacy, or mess in our business. It's not always easy, however, to draw the lines once they've been crossed. And sometimes, usually within the family, when what was once age-appropriate guidance has morphed meddling in the affairs of another adult.

Dictating what your boundaries are rarely does the job. An emotionally needy person will still make demands on your time; someone with a dominant personality is not going to stop trying to take over your life; a close friend or relative who feels entitled to tell you what to do may indulge you for a while, but then go right back to what she's always done.

Living your boundaries works. Rather than trying to push against others, get used to standing up for yourself, lovingly and kindly saying what you really mean, and sticking with your decisions. Gradually, you will start feeling better about yourself, which will bring you an air of self-confidence that wards off boundary-crossers.

No matter what you do, however, you're not going to redraw a long-standing pattern in a day. Little by little, though, you can determine a new design, one that respects you, and respects others, too, by not enabling them to continue their behavior—at least not with you.

*It's another way to look at it!*

# Where do you draw the line?

*Is "no" selfish or assertive?* If you go along with whatever others ask you to do or become involved in, despite your wants or needs, you're letting others take control of your life. If you say "no" when you mean "no," and "yes" when you mean "yes," you're protecting your time and taking responsibility for where you will direct your energy and efforts.

*Is putting the wishes of others first a sign of weakness or strength?* If you're secure in who you are, you have it within you to defer to the ideas, wishes, and plans of others, as they defer to yours. Healthy relationships are based on mutual give-and-take.

*Is insisting on your way authoritarianism or leadership?* If you're the one in charge—parent, guardian, teacher, manager—it's up to you to determine what goes on in your sphere of responsibility. You're accountable, so it's your job to assume a strong leadership role marked with wisdom, kindness, thoughtfulness, and respect.

*Is talking about your achievements boasting or informing?* When someone crosses the line on this one, you know it! Yet if you don't believe in your abilities enough to mention them, you are hiding an important part of yourself that could create relationships and opportunities. Avoid coming across as an ego-tripper by checking your motivation. Are you mentioning your achievements to attract applause, or help others get to know you better? To boost yourself above others, or show how you can contribute to the common good?

# Lines to draw...

*Places* you will go and with whom...what you will lend, for how long, and to whom...when you will insist on privacy...what you will tolerate and what you will protest.

*Questions* about yourself, your past, and your relationships that you will answer directly when asked; and questions you will refuse to answer unless required by someone with the authority to ask or the need to know.

*Responsibilities* that belong to you and those that belong to others...helpful, constructive criticism concerning your efforts, plans, or behavior; and unwarranted, mean-spirited comments.

*Physical expression* that makes you feel loved, cared for, and appreciated; and actions that leave you feeling uncomfortable, used, guilty, or wounded in body or soul.

*Relationships* that allow you to be yourself, to grow, to feel valued; and relationships that diminish or belittle you...that leave you feeling disrespected or used for the convenience of others.

*Draw the lines.*

# Quotable…

Lend yourself to others, but give yourself to yourself.
*Michel de Montaigne*

No one can make you feel inferior without
your consent.
*Eleanor Roosevelt*

He that respects himself is safe from others;
he wears a coat of mail that none can pierce.
*Henry Wadsworth Longfellow*

I do not wish women to have power over men;
but over themselves.
*Mary Wollstonecraft Shelley*

Never esteem anything as of advantage to you that will
make you break your word or lose your self-respect.
*Marcus Aurelius*

Borrowed thoughts, like borrowed money,
only show the poverty of the borrower.
*Marguerite Blessington*

There is just one life for each of us: our own.
*Euripides*

# What one man does, another fails to do…

Respect yourself, and others will respect you.

To love others, we must first learn to love ourselves.

If you put a small value upon yourself, rest assured that the world will not raise your price.

Who is not good for himself is no good for others, either.

Self-knowledge is the beginning of self-improvement.

Put your future in good hands—your own.

# …what's fit for me may not be fit for you.

# PLAYING BY THE RULES

Everybody!
In your places, please!

# Treat others...

*...the way you want them to treat you.* The Golden Rule has found expression in religious teachings, public ethics, and wise proverbs since ancient times. And ever since then, people of goodwill have heeded the advice and made it their standard in their relations with others.

Social conventions, like politeness, courtesy, and civility, stem from the Golden Rule. Whether in public or in private, no one appreciates being confronted with rudeness and insolence. Self-respect and respect for others go hand-in-hand, along with kind words and kindly responses; fair opinions and fair treatment; generosity to others and generosity in return.

Will it always work? No, because there are people who won't play by any rules. They're the ones who will cheat, even if no one has ever cheated them...who will push ahead no matter who's pushed back...who will give a rude answer in response to a polite and reasonable question. They're the same people, however, who bear the burden of empty relationships and leave behind a landscape of burned bridges and damaged roads.

The Golden Rule is the first rule of living well with yourself and among others. It's the golden pathway to friendship and fulfillment, genuine success and lasting peace of mind.

*It's another way to look at it!*

# Quotable...

He that does good to another does good also
to himself, not only in the consequence, but in
the very act. For the consciousness of well-doing
is in itself ample reward.
*Seneca*

Do not do to others what angers you if done to
you by others.
*Socrates*

Avoid doing what you would blame others for doing.
*Thales*

Sow good service; sweet remembrances will grow
from them.
*Madame de Staël*

All things whatsoever ye would that men should
do to you, do ye even so to them.
*Matthew 7:12*

# A little lift of laughter…

*Ooops!*

Little Meg rushed to her mother and said, "Tom broke my baby doll!"

"Oh, I'm so sorry, sweetheart," the sympathetic mom said. "How did it happen?"

"It happened when I hit him over the head with it."

*Not That Easy*

A city slicker thought he'd have an easy time passing his phony eighteen-dollar bills in a small town's country store. When he found what he thought would be an easy target, he entered and handed one of the bills to the clerk at the counter.

"Can I get change for this?" he asked.

"Sure," said the clerk. "Would you like two nines or three sixes?"

*Act of Kindness*

During a particularly cold winter, a construction foreman noticed that one of his workmen wasn't wearing earmuffs. Knowing that the man was having financial difficulties, the foreman decided he'd do the right thing and buy the man a pair. The man thanked him, but on the next day—even more bitter than the last—the foreman asked the man why he wasn't wearing them.

"Well, sir," the man explained, "because after I put them on yesterday, somebody offered to buy me lunch, and I didn't hear him. Never again, never again!"

## …to help along the way!

*Do all the good you can...*
You know how good it feels when you meet someone who makes you feel good. Warmth, friendliness, acceptance, gentleness, kindness, and love make others feel good, too.

*By all the means you can,*
*In all the ways you can...*
Like the gifts of warm thoughts...gentle words...positive encouragements...generous giving...helpful hands...feet that are willing to walk with a friend on a difficult path.

*In all the places you can...*
In school and the workplace...while driving and shopping...during meetings and gatherings...as you stroll in the park and walk in the city...while standing in line and sitting in waiting rooms...among friends and strangers...and most especially, at home.

*At all the times you can.*
John Wesley

# Help another's boat across...

What goes around, comes around.

A clear conscience is a soft pillow.

Those who set their minds on virtue will do no evil.

Practicing the Golden Rule is not a sacrifice; it is an investment.

Happy are those who conduct themselves honorably.

Character is easier kept than recovered.

## ...and yours will reach the shore.

# LAUGHING
# ALL THE WAY

Hardy-har-har!
That made my day!

# Many things are decidedly not funny...

*...but there's humor in almost anything.* Some people are good at finding it, and if you're one of those people, you possess a priceless gift.

You're able to diffuse arguments with a gentle remark that lifts tension and opens time for emotions to cool and calmness to prevail. With your warm smile and welcome laughter, you help others see beyond their present problems and look at the bright side, and that's how trouble decreases and happiness increases.

Humor gives life balance, because no matter how bad things seem or how sad we feel, a touch of humor relieves hopelessness and sorrow, lightens burdens, and makes going forward possible. Many find that a good dose of laughter provides needed relaxation of mind and body, and better equips them to tackle tough, unfunny circumstances.

But most important of all is the ability—and the willingness—to laugh at ourselves. Laughter cuts big egos down to size and keeps pride in check. Self-importance isn't possible when we can admit our foibles and laugh. Laughter is the mark of self-awareness and self-confidence; the light of humility and wisdom; the result of peace within ourselves and peace with others; the sign of a heart filled with the hardy-har-har of living.

*It's another way to look at it!*

## Lord, Grant Me Humor

Lord, grant me a sense of humor
To smooth out the rough spots of life
And keep me from tension and anger,
Bad temper, complaining, and strife.

Let me be the one who offers
The comment that brings on the grins,
The insight that finds in our losses
Our blessings and myriad wins.

It's humor that eases sorrows
And lets in the sunshine each day—
It's laughter the heart will remember
When troubles have long passed away.

*Patricia Mitchell*

# Live to laugh…

What soap is to the body laughter is to the soul.

Even if there's nothing to laugh about, laugh on credit.

Laughter adds years to your life, and life to your years.

Those who laugh, last.

There's nothing more wonderfully contagious than laughter.

A good laugh and a long sleep are the best cures in the doctor's book.

If you're too busy to laugh, you're too busy.

Laughter is the music of the soul.

## …and laugh to live.

# A little lift of laughter...

*Last Laugh*

A husband and wife were staying at a lodge in Alaska, something the husband had long wanted to do. Gazing at the majestic scenery from their balcony, the husband exclaimed, "This is paradise! I can picture us living in a cabin up here off the grid, where I could fish and hunt moose, and we could drive a dog team instead of a car!" Hearing no response from his wife, the man turned to her and said, "Honey, honestly, what would you miss if we moved out here permanently?"

"You," she replied.

*Short-Lived Joy*

One morning, the drill sergeant addressed his group of new recruits by saying, "Today, I have good news and bad news. The good news is that Private Stephens will be setting the pace for our morning run." Murmurs of delight arose from the group, because Private Stephens, slow and out of shape, was always the last one to finish. "Now for the bad news," the sergeant continued. "Private Stephens will be driving a truck."

*A good laugh is like manure to a farmer—*
*it doesn't do any good until you spread it around.*

# Quotable…

A good laugh is sunshine in a house.
*William Makepeace Thackeray*

Men show their character in nothing more clearly than by what they think laughable.
*Johann von Goethe*

Humor brings insight and tolerance.
*Agnes Repplier*

A person without a sense of humor is like a wagon without springs—jolted by every pebble in the road.
*Henry Ward Beecher*

Laughing is the sensation of feeling good all over and showing it principally in one place.
*Josh Billings*

Laughter…unfreezes pride and unwinds secrecy; it makes men forget themselves in the presence of something greater than themselves.
*G. K. Chesterton*

# CHOOSING THE BEST

Aaah...life is good
when you're the king of beasts.

# Choosing the best in life...

*...costs no money at all.* What it costs, though, is a desire to know what the best really is, and the discipline to choose it. Discipline? Yes, because the best things in life include joy, peace, faith, sharing, forgiveness, and love for others. And those aren't ready-made, off-the-shelf items, but qualities that grow as they're practiced day after day, and ripen as they become habits of a lifetime.

For instance, it's difficult for a heart filled with anger or bitterness to know joy, and impossible for one inflicted with greed to know peace or contentment. A life lived without faith in God is one ruled by personal reason and whims, and unlikely to bring fulfillment over the course of time. Without forgiveness, long-term friendships dwindle; and without genuine love for others, loneliness is never far behind.

Joy, peace, faith, sharing, forgiveness, and love... what would you add to the list? For any worthwhile quality, characteristic, or circumstance you choose as the best, chances are it's going to cost some effort—but when you're committed to choosing the best for yourself, cost is not what you're focused on. You're seeing, choosing, working for—and getting—the best.

*It's another way to look at it!*

# The best choices are…

*Enduring faith* to give your life meaning and purpose… to lift your eyes to things higher than yourself…to carry you through life's toughest times…to open your sight to the dawn even in the darkest of nights.

*Heartfelt gratitude* to shield you from the agony of jealousy and covetousness…to put your problems in perspective…to engender humility and generosity… to fill you with delight in what you have been given… to open the way for all that is good.

*Optimistic thoughts* to keep despair at bay…to create an upbeat, can-do attitude…to point your words and actions toward good results and positive outcomes…to envision a fulfilling life for you and lead you to it.

*Cheerful giving* to prevent selfishness and greed…to exercise control over personal desires and material things…to experience the joy of helping others…to know the rewards of sharing your abilities, resources, and blessings.

*Realistic expectations* to promote clear thinking and avoid self-delusion…to acknowledge your weaknesses and limitations…to equip you with a true-to-life vision of your potential…to enable you to put your efforts and attention on being the best you can be.

*Disciplined conduct* to lessen the impact of whim, emotion, and impulse on your words and actions...to not allow short-term pleasures to undermine long-term goals...to help you meet your responsibilities every day...to reap the many benefits of possessing integrity, maturity, and wisdom.

*Genuine friends* to support and encourage you along life's way...to accompany you through good times and bad...to show you the joys of being with others... to bless your life with fun, delight, and laughter...to return to you the love and companionship you give to them.

*Ethical principles* to set high standards and prompt you to meet them...guide you on the path of honesty, goodness, fairness, and truthfulness...to teach you how to forgive others and receive forgiveness...to show you the right thing to do and give you the desire to do it.

*Earned self-esteem* to equip you with the confidence that makes continued success possible...to create belief in yourself and your proven abilities...to make you less reliant on the criticisms, views, and opinions of others...to move you forward on the basis of objective achievements.

*Inner peace* to keep you from anxiety, fear, and panic when things aren't going right...to build in you a core of strength you can hold onto in any situation...to create in you a place of rest and quietness within that will always be there for you.

*Adopt* lasting values over temporary trends...worthwhile dreams over ephemeral wishes.

*Pursue* a single worthwhile goal over countless aims...one direction at a time over numerous wandering paths.

*Make things happen* rather than wait for things to happen to you...claim your goal, and then work toward it.

*Stand up* to challenges, whether they come in the form of physical disability, adverse circumstances, or difficult people...never let them intimidate you, but face them down with courage.

*Admit when you're wrong*...make amends where you can...accept the lesson you've learned...forgive yourself.

*Give generously* of your time, your effort, your resources, yourself...never demand a reward, but receive the grace of knowing you are one who blesses, one who makes a difference, one who loves.

*Celebrate* small successes achieved over big dreams unfulfilled...the person you really are over shaping yourself to the demands of others.

*Live joyfully...*
    *give abundantly...*
        *choose wisely...*
            *think positively.*

# Quotable…

Choose always the way that seems best, however rough it may be; custom will soon render it easy and agreeable.

*Pythagoras*

God asks no man whether he will accept life.
That is not the choice. You must take it.
The only choice is how.

*Henry Ward Beecher*

In each action we must look beyond the action at our past, present and future state, and at others whom it affects, and see the relations of all those things. And then we shall be very cautious.

*Blaise Pascal*

Someone once asked me what I regarded as the three most important requirements for happiness. My answer was: "A feeling that you have been honest with yourself and those around you; a feeling that you have done the best you could both in your personal life and in your work; and the ability to love others."

*Eleanor Roosevelt*

# TAKING ADVANTAGE
# OF ADVERSITY

Mama told me
there'd be days like this!

# Does it matter...

*...what you call adversity?* To find your answer, focus on these three words: Trouble. Hardship. Difficulties. The words alone bring on tension! But how about this trio of words? Experience. Growth. Opportunity. Now your mind relaxes a little, ready to entertain interesting, engaging possibilities.

Experience, growth, and opportunity describe the "other side" of adversity, but unless you look, you may not find, or be able to take advantage of, all that adversity provides. Test the theory by recalling a past setback or difficult circumstance you have endured. What specific life experiences, coping skills, and insights did you gain? Remember how much you learned about yourself, other people, and the way the world works by going through what you did. Had the incident never occurred, you would be less spiritually strong, less emotionally robust, and less knowledgeable than you are today.

Yes, bad things happen, and it's healthy to call them exactly what they are—bad! Yuck! But with every bad thing, there comes a multitude of good things, and it's healthy to call them exactly what they are, too—experience, growth, and opportunity. Those are more than good—they're life itself!

*It's another way to look at it!*

# Quotable...

Adversity has ever been considered as the state in which a man most easily becomes acquainted with himself, then, especially, being free from flatterers.
*Samuel Johnson*

Difficulties are meant to rouse, not discourage. The human spirit is to grow strong by conflict.
*William Ellery Channing*

All sorts of spiritual gifts come through privations, if they are accepted.
*Janet Erskine Stuart*

Some minds seem almost to create themselves, springing up under every disadvantage and working their solitary but irresistible way through a thousand obstacles.
*Washington Irving*

Never to suffer would never to have been blessed.
*Edgar Allan Poe*

Our real blessings often appear to us in the shape of pains, losses, and disappointments; but let us have patience, and we soon shall see them in their proper figures.
*Joseph Addison*

# When the ride gets rough...

*...slow down.* Postpone as many activities as you can, and delegate as many responsibilities and obligations as you're able.

*...keep your eyes on the road.* Unemotionally and objectively, define the present conditions and assess the extent of the damage being done.

*...look at a map.* Sometimes it's better to keep driving in the same direction, yet with added care and caution. Other times circumstances force you to turn around and go back to where you started...or take a turn-off and head in another direction...or stop and wait until rescue arrives.

*...call for help.* Within your circle of family and friends, coworkers and associates, there's someone who has experience fixing financial problems...navigating through medical issues...rebuilding a life after devastating loss.

*...don't give up on the trip,* because you're the "help" others are going to call when they're stranded by the side of the road. You'll understand where they are... you'll know what to do. You've been on rough rides before.

# Trouble brings experience...

No one knows better what is good than he who
has endured bad.

To turn an obstacle to one's advantage is a great
step toward victory.

Adversity is the only diet that will reduce a fat head.

Advise and counsel him; if he does not listen,
let adversity teach him.

God takes you to deep waters not to drown you,
but to show you how to swim.

The diamond cannot be polished without friction,
nor the man perfected without trials.

# ...and experience
# brings wisdom.

# The other side of the coin...

Prosperity is not without many fears and distastes, and adversity is not without comforts and hopes.

*Francis Bacon*

Adversity has the effect of eliciting talents, which, in prosperous circumstances, would have lain dormant.

*Horace*

Prosperity is a great teacher; adversity is a greater. Possession pampers the mind; privation trains and strengthens it.

*William Hazlitt*

Emergencies have always been necessary to progress. It was darkness which produced the lamp. It was fog that produced the compass. It was hunger that drove us to exploration. And it took a depression to teach us the real value of a job.

*Victor Hugo*

The good things that belong to prosperity are to be wished, but the good things that belong to adversity are to be admired.

*Seneca*

# SPEAKING OF WORDS

How does
"cockle-doodle-doo"
sound to you?

# Words have power...

*...tremendous power.* While everyone has heard the old saying, "Sticks and stones may break my bones, but words will never hurt me," few believe it. Who among us has not felt the sting of an unkind remark, barbed comment, or derogatory reference? Words are powerful!

Yet the same power that gives words their ability to hurt also enables them to heal. Sincere, heartfelt words mend friendships, comfort tears, and smooth the way ahead. Kind, thoughtful words build relationships, enhance trust, and bring hope to the lives of others. Complimentary, approving words build confidence and set the tone for further progress and satisfaction.

Despite the awesome power of words, most of us give little thought to them when we speak. We're so accustomed to talking—we do it every day!—that we rarely stop to listen to ourselves speak. Perhaps we're using harsh words where gentler would be better... careless words that are leaving unintended harm... or no words when someone hasn't heard a kind one all day.

Words matter. Which ones we choose, where and to whom we say them, and the tone of voice we use to speak them combine to make them powerful instruments. What are people hearing from you these days?

*It's another way to look at it!*

# Hear much...

One kind word has more power within it than
a dozen ultimatums.

A word out of season can mar a whole lifetime.

To talk without thinking is to shoot without aiming.

Water and words—easy to pour, but impossible to
recover.

To speak much is one thing; to speak well is another.

Always keep your words soft and sweet in case
the day comes you have to eat them.

## ...speak little.

# Quotable...

Positive words possess power. Words vibrate according to their character and nature. A negative word depresses, discourages and weakens us if we use it and dwell upon it.
*Henry Thomas Hamblin*

Once a word has been allowed to escape, it cannot be recalled.
*Horace*

Kind words produce their own image in men's souls; and a beautiful image it is.
*Blaise Pascal*

A very great part of the mischiefs that vex this world arises from words.
*Edmund Burke*

The rule of friendship means there should be mutual sympathy between them, each supplying what the other lacks and trying to benefit the other, always using friendly and sincere words.
*Cicero*

Discretion in speech is more than eloquence.
*Francis Bacon*

# Punny Words...

Easy chair – a hard chair to find empty

Window shopping – eye browsing

Halo – angel's greeting

Eyeglass maker – job that's a real grind

Backyard birdhouse – cheep motel

Yodeling – slope opera

Farmer – down-to-earth person

Diet – a triumph of mind over platter.

Credit card – buy pass

Acorn – an oak in a nutshell

Funniest animal – a stand-up chameleon

Bread baker – one who has all the dough

Greed – state of mine

Carpet – flooring bought by the yard
and worn by the foot

# A little lift of laughter…

*Thanks for Asking*

A highway patrol officer noticed a woman driving down the highway at top speed, all the while busily knitting. He revved his motorcycle, caught up with her, and motioned for her to roll down her window. When she did, he yelled, "Pull over!"

"No, officer," she shouted back, "mittens!"

*Decisions*

A farmer told his neighbor that he was trying to decide whether to buy a bicycle or a cow for his farm. His neighbor said, "Pretty easy. You can't ride a cow into town, can you?"

"Nope," the farmer replied, "but you can't milk a bicycle in the barn, either."

# …to help along the way!

# MOVING FORWARD

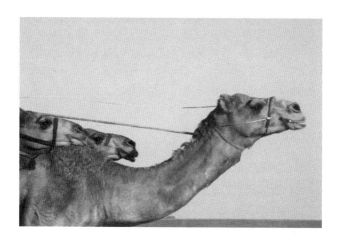

Ready or not,
here we come!

# Have you ever driven a car in the snow...

*...and gotten stuck in a drift?* The wheels spin and spin, but they can get no traction in the slushy mess!

Sometimes, the daily routine of life can make us feel as if we're stuck in a snowbank. Even though we're working hard and our calendar is bursting with events and activities, we aren't making any discernable progress. We realize that, while busy, we're not truly engaged in what we're doing, and we've lost a lot of our old enthusiasm.

If you know the feeling, it's time to get unstuck. You don't need to revamp your whole lifestyle to regain a sense of purpose and pleasure, but only add a little sunshine here and there. Anything that shakes up your day's routine can help–a lunchtime walk, an evening visit with a good friend, a weekend spent doing something you've been putting off for a long time, or have never done before.

A few warm rays are all it takes to turn that car-stopping snow drift into rivulets of water that sparkle in the sunshine. Ready or not, world, here you come!

*It's another way to look at it!*

*Renew* your pleasure in life by doing at least one small thing every day that delights you. It need serve no other purpose than to bring warmth to your heart and a smile to your face. What would do that for you right now? And if you're way too busy to do it, you're way too busy!

*Redecorate* the interior of your heart. Sweep out shadowy fears darkening your outlook and negative thoughts cluttering your mind. Get rid of musty "musts" taking up so much of your time and energy. Fling open the windows of your being! Breathe fresh air of hope, optimism, and faith in the goodness of God.

*Relive* good times you have shared with others, and remember all the wonderful people who have touched your life in both big and small ways. Call to mind those who have helped you, encouraged you, and cared for you...and especially those who have made you laugh. Send a warm thought to each!

*Recount* the blessings you enjoy today. Name each one, starting with the gift of a brand new day. Include not only your many material possessions, the sight of another's smile...the touch of a loved one's hand in yours...the taste of a sweet or savory morsel on your tongue...the fragrance of a newly opened blossom... the sound of a sublime musical composition.

*Restore* the zest of the moment by concentrating on the moment. Set your sights not on the big picture, but on whatever it is you're doing today. Today's activities are signs of your ability to do, contribute, participate, and take this one small step forward.

*Reconnect* with meaningful and worthwhile values and principles. If something you are doing falls short of your ideals, take action to remove that activity or circumstance from your life. Mark and celebrate those places in your life where you are putting your principles into practice.

*Re-create* the structure of your day wherever possible. Where there's little or no flexibility on the outside, restructure the inside by approaching your day with a new attitude. Commit yourself to enthusiasm, act enthusiastically, and you will feel enthusiastic about what you're doing.

*Rejoice* in the progress you make each day, because you *are* making progress! Each small task done well, each word spoken kindly, each hand offered in assistance is a small step in the journey of a life well-lived.

# Yard by yard, it's very hard...

It's better to do a little good today than dream
of doing a great good someday.

Even little stars shine in the darkness.

Some people dream of doing something;
others wake up and do it.

It's great to have your feet on the ground;
but you need to keep them moving.

# ...but inch by inch,
# it's a cinch!

# Quotable...

Even if you're on the right track,
you'll get run over if you just sit there.
*Will Rogers*

If you only keep adding little by little,
it will soon become a big heap.
*Hesiod*

Great things are not done by impulse,
but by a series of small things brought together.
*Vincent van Gogh*

Success depends in a very large measure
upon individual initiative and exertion,
and cannot be achieved except by dint of hard work.
*Anna Pavlova*

Practice yourself in little things, for heaven's sake,
and thence proceed to greater.
*Epictetus*

He who moves not forward goes backward.
*Johann von Goethe*

# CELEBRATING YOU

Lookin' good, if I do say so myself…
and I do!

# Are you happy with who you see…

*…when you look into a mirror?* While your inner qualities are of supreme importance, your outer qualities are what greet you in the bathroom mirror every day…and the first thing people see whenever they meet you.

Though our culture certainly puts too much emphasis on appearance, we know from our own experience that appearance counts. Take, for example, someone who looks like she doesn't care about herself. Why would we think she'd care about us, either? Chances are, we wouldn't stay around long enough to discover her wonderful (or not-so-wonderful) inner qualities!

As we grow from one life stage to the next, and as we assume new roles and positions in life, it's good to make sure our appearance is working for us, and not against us. Good posture, clean and healthy skin, updated hair style, becoming makeup, and appropriate clothing all serve to make us look good. And when we look good, we feel good…and when we feel good, we're more apt to radiate warmth and confidence… and there's nothing like warmth and confidence to heighten our chances of success and attract the attention of people.

Stand in front of a mirror and meet yourself for the first time. Lookin' good?

*It's another way to look at it!*

# To improve your appearance at any age…

Use your *lips* to speak words of kindness, gentleness, and thoughtfulness.

Use your *eyes* to see the best in yourself and others, in events and circumstances.

Use your *ears* to listen patiently and attentively to those who speak to you.

Use your *mind* to think pleasant thoughts and think of ways to change things for the better.

Use your *hands* to touch, caress, help, and comfort.

Use your *feet* to visit the lonely, assist the needy, and go where you're most needed.

Use your *heart* to cherish yourself and those you love.

# Quotable...

Know first who you are; and then adorn yourself accordingly.
*Euripides*

How things look on the outside of us depends on how things are on the inside of us.
*Henry Ward Beecher*

The world is governed more by appearance than realities, so that it is fully as necessary to seem to know something as to know it.
*Daniel Webster*

Appearances are a glimpse of the unseen.
*Aeschylus*

# A little lift of laughter…

*Beauty Regimen*

A little girl was watching as her mother smoothed cold cream over her face and neck. "Why are you doing that, Mommy?" the child asked.

"To make myself beautiful," the woman replied. Then she took a tissue and began to wipe the cream off her skin.

"What's wrong, Mommy," said the girl, "are you giving up already?"

*Makes Sense*

A young woman was an hour late returning to work from lunch. The boss asked her where she had been.

"Getting my hair cut," she answered.

"On company time?" he shouted.

"Well, it grew on company time, didn't it?" she said.

"Not all of it!"

"I didn't get all of it cut off."

*That Explains It*

A woman was at the bus stop when a man came and stood next to her. She noticed that he had stamped envelopes arranged in a neat design all over his bare head. After a few minutes, she could stand it no longer, and asked, "I mean no offense, but why do you have stamped envelopes arranged all over your head?"

"Oh, no offense taken, ma'am," the man replied. "It's mail pattern baldness."

## …to help along the way!

*Exercise is a great idea, except...*

> ...my favorite machine at the gym is the
> vending machine.
> ...if God had intended me to touch my toes,
> He would have put them up around my knees.
> ...I get winded just thinking about a mile run.
> ...I consider myself in good shape. Round is a
> good shape.

*It's time to diet if...*

> ...you can pinch an inch—on your forehead.
> ...you're in the market for a whole new wardrobe
> of bigger clothes.
> ...your idea of burning off fat is eating a pizza
> in a sauna.
> ...the chair gets up when you do.
> ...you believe that gravy is a beverage.
> ...you carry your weight well, but it takes two trips.

*You know you're in a health-food store when...*

> ...even the flies are doing push-ups.
> ...everything is labeled "natural," but you want
> all the preservatives you can get.

# BLESSING OTHERS

I'm squeal-ly glad
our paths crossed.

# Each of us has received from others...

*...and each of us has the privilege of giving to others.* Yes, it's not simply a duty to see to the needs of others, but a privilege to bless lives where, when, and how we can.

Though sometimes we're able to bless with the gift of money to a person, family, or organization in need, there's an even more important gift, and it's something all of us can give every day—the gift of ourselves. All it takes is a willingness to remain aware of those around us, to focus our attention on them, and to make their well-being our first priority.

There are few people whose day isn't brightened by a warm smile or a friendly greeting. Just think of the many times the helpfulness of a store clerk or the kindness of a passerby has blessed an otherwise ordinary day! That's the kind of difference you can make in the day of someone else just by giving the gift of yourself.

Today, give the best gift of all. Offer a warm smile and a kindly word. Share a moment of friendship with someone else, and show how much you care about them as a unique individual. Every day you have the opportunity—no, the privilege!—of blessing the heart of another person.

*It's another way to look at it!*

# Pass It On!

*Have you had a kindness shown?*
*Pass it on!*
*'Twas not given for thee alone—*
*Pass it on!*
*Let it travel down the years,*
*Let it wipe another's tears,*
*Till in Heaven the deed appears—*
*Pass it on!*

Henry Burton

*Bless a life today!* Tell a hurting heart how much you care...take the extra time to hear another's pain... whisper the three little words that mean the most into a loved one's ear.

*Use your skills and talents to* provide what others lack...see a need and ask what you can do to help... remember those whose lives are shadowed with grief and loss.

*Notice others' concerns and cares...*help in real and practical ways...offer encouragement and support...let them know you're there for them.

*Ask a neighbor how she's doing...*remind a friend of how much fun you've had together...reach out to someone who recently has joined your social circle.

*Pray a prayer of thanksgiving* for those whose words or actions have lightened your load and brought a smile to your face...*and bless a life today!*

# Giving begins with an open heart…

We keep only that which we give away.

Give to the world the best you have,
and the best will come back to you.

A bit of fragrance always clings to the hand
that gives you roses.

You cannot always have happiness,
but you can always give it to others.

Those who do not give until they're asked
have waited too long.

## …and ends with an open hand.

# Quotable...

It is in giving oneself that one receives.
*Francis of Assisi*

What do we live for if it is not to make life less
difficult for each other?
*George Eliot*

We should give as we would receive, cheerfully,
quickly, and without hesitation; for there is no
grace in a benefit that sticks to the fingers.
*Seneca*

If I can stop one heart from breaking, I shall not
live in vain.
*Emily Dickinson*

Blessed are those who can give without remembering
and take without forgetting.
*Elizabeth Bibesco*

We cannot live only for ourselves. A thousand
fibers connect us with our fellow men.
*Herman Melville*

The only true gift is a portion of thyself.
*Ralph Waldo Emerson*

# PRAISING THE DAY

Seal it with gratitude...

# We respond to praise…

*…mind and body, heart and soul.* Who among us doesn't feel at least a prick of pleasure when we hear someone admire what we've accomplished? Who would want to remain indifferent to a loved one's appreciation for the person we are? There's nothing like a round of applause to lighten the heart and brighten the day!

Praise blesses those who offer praise, too. Those who praise others create an atmosphere of harmony, encouragement, and goodwill; and everyone benefits from the warmth in the room. When you take time to notice and praise what's around you—flowers in bloom, clear skies above, the reflection of a skyscraper on a rain-washed sidewalk—and suddenly the world looks full of beautiful things to enjoy. Praise the day, and it seems that the hours themselves respond by bringing you even more reason to be happy and give thanks.

Open your day with a word of praise for who you are, where you are, and all the opportunities in front of you. Give thanks for the blessings you possess, along with your skills and abilities, your hopes and desires. Wrap yourself in gratitude for the people you love and who love you. In everything, give praise, and praise is what returns to you.

*It's another way to look at it!*

# Quotable...

When you arise in the morning, think of what
a precious privilege it is to be alive—to breathe,
to think, to enjoy, to love.
*Marcus Aurelius*

Let the thankful heart sweep through the day and,
as the magnet finds the iron, so it will find,
in every hour, some heavenly blessings!
*Henry Ward Beecher*

In the deepest night of trouble and sorrow,
God gives us so much to be thankful for that
we need never cease our singing.
*Samuel Taylor Coleridge*

When I first open my eyes upon the morning
meadows and look out upon the beautiful world,
I thank God I am alive.
*Ralph Waldo Emerson*

We must give ourselves more earnestly and
intelligently and generously than we have to
the happy duty of appreciation.
*Mariana Griswold van Rensselaer*

*If anyone would tell you*
*the shortest, surest way*
*to all happiness and all perfection,*
*he must tell you to make it a rule*
*to yourself to thank and praise*
*God for everything that*
*happens to you. For it is certain*
*that whatever calamity happens to you,*
*if you thank and praise God for it,*
*you turn it into a blessing.*

William Law

# Some people complain because God put thorns on roses…

The wise count their blessings;
fools, their problems.

If you can't be thankful for what you have,
be thankful for what you have escaped.

Seeds of discouragement cannot grow in a
thankful heart.

Those who forget the language of thankfulness
can never get on speaking terms with happiness.

Who does not thank for little will not thank
for much.

## …while others praise Him for putting roses among thorns.

*Imagine…*

…you have just finished the most delicious dinner you have ever eaten, and now you want to tell your friend about it. You call her on the phone, and she answers. With excitement and eagerness in your voice, you tell her about the meal—the aroma that made your mouth water the moment you sat down at the table…the attractive and appetizing appearance of each dish…the savory taste of your favorite flavors and spices on your tongue…the feeling of contentment and satisfaction when you had finished. You mention your praise for the chef's skill and expertise, and your gratitude for the delightful, pleasurable mealtime event.

*Imagine…*

…ending each day as if it were the best you have ever experienced. With gratitude filling your heart, talk about the day—the fragrance of a springtime breeze or the smell of logs crackling in the fireplace on a winter's evening…the awesome splendor of a sunrise or sunset, a fluffy white cloud or a starry night…the sweet taste of a compliment, the smiling face of a long-time friend…the satisfaction of what went right and worked out well for you…your praise to God, the author and creator of it all.

*Imagine!*

# LOOKING UP

I'm telling ya—
Someone's up there, all right!

# Caring for your soul...

*...is as important as caring for your body.* When you
don't eat right, get little sleep, or neglect to exercise,
you're not at your best, right? You feel listless and out
of sorts, and you're vulnerable to every cough and
sneeze going around! Similarly, your emotional and
spiritual health hinges on how much nourishment you
give your soul.

At the center of soul-full health is faith in a loving,
forgiving, and powerful God. Faith in God's love for
you provides a sense of dignity and self-worth, even if
others attempt to pull you down. Faith in God's forgiveness removes inner turmoil, replacing guilt with peace
of mind and heart. Faith in God's power opens you to
ability, authority, and knowledge beyond what you can
see and understand. With faith, you discover what it
means to live purposefully, abundantly, and joyfully.

Daily times of reflection, meditation, and prayer put
you in touch with God and deepen your relationship
with Him. He promises to feed your soul with the rich-
est of foods—wisdom, guidance, and grace.

You are blessed with a body and blessed with a soul.
Both need—and deserve—daily TLC.

*It's another way to look at it!*

# Quotable...

The first condition of human goodness is something
to love; the second, something to revere.
*George Eliot*

It is the heart which experiences God, and not reason.
This, then, is faith: God felt by heart, not by reason.
*Blaise Pascal*

Faith is an excitement and an enthusiasm: it is a
condition of intellectual magnificence to which we
must cling as to treasure, and not squander in the
small coin of empty words.
*George Sand*

It is impossible to live a life of faith without
prayer—continual prayer. It is only through
persistence and perseverance in prayer that
our faith can be maintained.
*Henry Thomas Hamblin*

Faith is to believe what you do not see;
the reward of this faith is to see what you believe.
*Augustine*

*When your faith is tested with trials,* do not lose your faith, but lean more heavily on it. Your faith in God's power to lead will take you through…your hope for a better tomorrow will get you there.

*When your faith is tested with doubt,* do not give in to doubt, but delve more deeply into faith. Read, discover, pray. Open the eyes of your soul to those things that cannot be seen, yet are real, lasting, and true.

*When your faith is tested with mockery,* do not let the wounds destroy you, but be glad! You are not being spiritual, but acting spiritually. You're not simply talking about faith, but walking according to your convictions, and everyone can see.

*When your faith is tested with mystery,* do not cloud your faith, but relax in the awe and incomprehensibility of God's abundant blessings, His open forgiveness, His steady presence, and His unchanging love for you.

# When at night you cannot sleep…

Prayer may not change the circumstances,
but it changes the one who prays.

God loves to get knee-mail.

A problem not worth praying about is not
worth worrying about.

Knowing a prayer by heart isn't important;
saying a prayer with the heart is.

Joy and thankfulness are the secret ingredients
to all effective prayer.

God invites us to burden Him with whatever
burdens us.

## …talk to the Shepherd;
## stop counting sheep.

*To leap across an abyss,*
*one is better served by faith than doubt.*
William James

Faith gives you the confidence to try, because
you know that, no matter where or how you land,
God is there.

*Fear knocked at the door.*
*Faith answered, and no one was there.*
Proverb

Faith provides courage to leave the safe boundaries
of routine and familiarity, because you know that
He is never more than a prayer away.

*I would rather walk with God*
*in the dark than go alone in the light.*
Mary Gardiner Brainard

Faith brings willingness to travel through tough
times, because you choose His will over your
plans...His wisdom over your knowledge...His
guidance over your preference in all things.

# RAISING THE BAR

How high can you go? REACH...

# There's a difference between excellence...

*...and perfection.* Those who strive for excellence are constantly on the look-out for places where they can do just a little bit better, and they do it. Those who insist on perfection, however, consign themselves to a frustrating course. Complete perfection isn't possible, and they exhaust themselves trying to reach for it.

Excellence energizes you with ongoing aims that require you to reach, learn, and grow. In doing so, you're rewarded with the satisfaction accomplishment brings, even if only a single small step forward was possible. Experience with excellence shows you where to put your best efforts, leaving what's inconsequential behind so you can focus on what's important.

When your eyes are on excellence, you're not afraid to rise to the next level, because you've proven to yourself that you're able to climb...you're not held back by obstacles, because you're not accustomed to stopping where they are...you're not afraid of hard work, because you know that's the only way excellence was ever achieved by anyone.

Most of us know how to get by. Few of us take the initiative to place the bar higher, and then reach up for it in thought, word, and action.

*It's another way to look at it!*

*I am not bound to win,*
*but I am bound to be true.*
*I am not bound to succeed,*
*but I am bound to live up to*
*what light I have.*

Abraham Lincoln


*On God for all events depend;*
*You cannot want when God's your friend.*
*Weigh well your part and do your best;*
*Leave to your Maker all the rest.*

Nathaniel Cotton


*It is easy enough to be pleasant*
*When life flows by like a song.*
*But the man worthwhile is the one who will smile*
*When everything goes dead wrong.*

Ella Wheeler Wilcox

# Good, better, best— never let it rest…

People who seek perfection in their lives are setting themselves up for failure.

Those who claim it cannot be done should not interrupt those doing it.

Those who want a perfect friend are bound to remain friendless.

Excellence comes before work only in the dictionary.

Those who sow mediocrity, reap mediocrity; those who sow excellence, reap excellence.

Excellence is measured by the willingness to keep reaching.

# …until your good is better and your better is best.

# Quotable...

Next to excellence is the appreciation of it.
*William Makepeace Thackeray*

It is reasonable to have perfection in our eye that we
may always advance toward it, though we know it can
never be reached.
*Samuel Johnson*

Excellence encourages one about life generally;
it shows the spiritual wealth of the world.
*George Eliot*

We are what we repeatedly do. Excellence,
then, is not an act, but a habit.
*Aristotle*

We should not judge people by their peak
of excellence; but by the distance they have
traveled from the point where they started.
*Henry Ward Beecher*

Life's like a play: it's not the length,
but the excellence of the acting that matters.
*Seneca*

*Picture excellence!* In one specific instance you can recall, picture yourself responding not the way you did, but with excellence. This is the time you say the right thing...do the right thing. It didn't happen then, but next time it can. What do you need to change to make this picture a reality?

*Picture excellence!* It means observable change. Your perspective changes immediately, and your actions follow. It might take time for others to realize that this isn't just a short-term spurt of idealism, but the way it's going to be from here on out.

*Picture excellence*—and picture it again! Frame it. Put it where you will see it every day, and live it. Own excellence, make it real in your life, and excellence will be yours.

# STRESSING LESS

Stress? Stress? What, me stress?

# Being busy is good...

*...but it's possible you're busier than is good for you.*
How long has it been since you've had a full night's
sleep? When did you take your last vacation—two, five,
ten years ago? Is sitting down for your meals the rule,
or an exception? How often do you spend an afternoon
doing something you love, just for the fun of it?

If you're too busy, you're well acquainted with
stress. It waits for you to wake up in the morning,
reminding you that you have one day to take care of
three days' work. It's there every evening, prompting
you to think about everything that's waiting for you
the next morning. Meanwhile, it's been with you all
headache-producing, stomach-churning day long!

Right now might be a busier-than-usual time for you,
yet you can still possess—and need—a heart-deep place
of peace. This place to go in mind and soul calms you
when things are hectic by refreshing your outlook,
replenishing your energy, and strengthening your ability to cope with the situation. When there's a place of
peace and stillness inside, what's going on outside has
little power to cause you stress.

Inner peace doesn't come naturally, but you can
cultivate it without much stress at all!

*It's another way of looking at it!*

# Cultivate a place of peace inside your heart...

When anxiety strikes, take time to describe what you are anxious about. Then ask yourself: Is anxiety helping the problem, or piling on stress? Will anxiety makes you more able to tackle the issue, or less?

Are your inner thoughts contributing to stress or to peace? Negative, offensive, and blaming comments you make to yourself are no more acceptable than those uttered to others. Declare your heart a positive-words-only zone. If an unfair, judgmental thought creeps in, send it back out again—pronto!

Is there a specific person or situation that causes you stress? If you can, distance yourself from the person or situation; if you can't, there's a place neither can enter without your permission—and that's your heart. Change your perception of the person by trying to understand his or her wants and needs. See the situation as a problem, but not a personal attack. Refuse to stress over what is beyond your power to change.

# For inner peace…

*… sitting in a fragrant garden* with birds singing over-head is nice, but not necessary. While a restful setting is conducive to peace, you don't need to depend on your surroundings when a place of peace exists within you.

*…ignoring problems* isn't satisfactory, because you care about your problems, your friends' problems, and the world's problems. It simply means that you know what you can and can't control…you take your responsibilities, but not yourself, seriously…and you trust God for the outcome.

*…spending hours in meditation* might work, yet you might not have the time or inclination to follow that route. A few minutes' calm reflection each day pro-motes calmer thinking, contributes to self-awareness, strengthens your relationship with God, and cultivates lasting inner peace.

# Don't hurry, don't worry...

The quieter you become,
the more you're able to hear.

Stress less—
resign as general manager of the universe.

Serenity is not freedom from the storm,
but peace amid the storm.

In acceptance,
there is peace.

No time is ever wasted that is spent
in wordless solitude.

True peace is in the present moment.

## ...do your best,
## then let it rest.

# Quotable...

Never be in a hurry; do everything quietly and in a
calm spirit. Do not lose your inner peace for anything
whatsoever, even if your whole world seems upset.
*Francis de Sales*

We must reserve a little back-shop, all our own,
entirely free, wherein to establish our true liberty and
principle retreat and solitude.
*Michel de Montaigne*

Nowhere can man find a quieter or more untroubled
retreat than in his own soul.
*Marcus Aurelius*

First keep the peace within yourself, then you can also
bring peace to others.
*Thomas à Kempis*

Nothing gives one person so much advantage over
another as to remain always cool and unruffled under
all circumstances.
*Thomas Jefferson*

Nothing can bring you peace but yourself.
*Ralph Waldo Emerson*

# SIMPLIFYING LIFE

Now, if only I could remember
where I hid those acorns…

# There are practical reasons...

*...to simplify your life.* Not the least of which, of course, is that you'll remember where you put things because you'll have fewer of them!

Now for other reasons. A simplified life is just plain simpler—not fettered with unnecessary involvements, complicated dealings, and convoluted aims. Examples: If you keep your finances simple, you understand where your money is and what it's doing. If you keep your interactions with others straightforward and aboveboard, you don't fear a tangle of bad consequences. If your goals are clear in your mind, you can take the best path to get there.

If you keep your possessions simple—that is, no excess, no newfangled gadget just because it's what other people are buying—you take pleasure in what you own and it's benefiting you. Also, fewer possessions means fewer appliances to maintain, or pay to have maintained; and that means more time and money to put toward experiences that really mean something to you.

As you practice simplification, you'll discover that your need to own, collect, and possess diminishes, and you're liberated from the pull of all those lively ads and colorful store flyers that drag you to buy more, more, and more.

Practical reasons...and spiritual reasons, too. You'll have more emotional time and space for the things that really matter.

*It's another way to look at it!*

# Seven Secrets of Simplicity

1. *Self-control*—Curb impulses that don't measure up to the person you want to be or the simpler life you want to pursue. In a short time, self-control becomes a habit; you won't feel deprived of anything, because those things that previously seemed necessary aren't appealing anymore.

2. *Contentment*—Commit to contentment. When tempted to envy another person's position or possessions, count your own blessings. Wish the other person well, and then be glad that you are you, a unique loved-by-God person with a special purpose to fulfill in this world. Desire contentment, and you will be content.

3. *Purpose*—Dedicate yourself to worthwhile work. What you are doing each day contributes to your well-being and the well-being of those dependent on you. With all that occupies your hours, you are honoring this day's opportunities and building toward your future.

4. *Wisdom*—Realize that accumulating things brings only temporary happiness. Once the moment has passed, happiness wears off, leaving you with an emptiness filled only with more things.

5. *Reverence*—Give honor to higher values and principles, those ancient and time-honored teachings that encourage you to set your mind on things above. Yes, here and now is important, but eternity is of immeasurable value.

6. *Generosity*—Share your resources with others in need. Selfless sharing rewards you with deep, lasting satisfaction; acquiring excess for yourself yields little pleasure.

7. *Dependence*—Rely on the goodness of God to carry you through. Everything doesn't depend on you; you can afford to relax...enjoy...and simplify.

# Quotable...

If you wish to give happiness, do not multiply
possessions, but reduce wants.
*Seneca*

The only simplicity that matters is the simplicity
of the heart.
*G. K. Chesterton*

I am bound to praise the simple life, because I have
lived it and found it good.
*John Burroughs*

Purity and simplicity are the two wings with which
man soars above the earth and all temporary nature.
*Thomas à Kempis*

A simple life is its own reward.
*George Santayana*

Simplicity, simplicity, simplicity! I say, let your affairs
be as two or three, and not a hundred or a thousand.
*Henry David Thoreau*

# Simplicity...

It's not a one-time project, but a way of living that is drawn to unpretentiousness, self-awareness, and contentment with who you are and where you are.

It doesn't mean you live in a cabin in the wilderness, but that you live without piling possessions one on top of another, as a bulwark against pain, insecurity, or misfortune.

It doesn't ask you to live stingily, but prudently, within your means and not in need of possessions to bolster your worth or self-esteem.

It never proposes that you do without, but do more within all that you are, all that you have, and all the potential that lies within you.

*Simplicity...*

## Positive ideas... healthful solutions... liberated living!

# RECEIVING COMFORT

I know how it feels.
Doggone it, I've been there!

# No matter what happens in your life…

*…there's someone else who knows how it feels.* Very likely, that someone is familiar to you—maybe your good friend— but you never realized that, years ago, she had experienced the same set-back… heard the same diagnosis…overcome the same addiction…faced the same tragedy.

Many of us are reluctant to share with others what has happened in the past. The reasons are many, including a desire to let bygones be bygones, protect the privacy of those involved, or put a positive face to the world. While these are good reasons not to reveal our personal sorrows every chance we get, there's one compelling time and place to do so, and that's to comfort someone who's grieving.

Whenever you're scared, confused, or unsure, turn toward those around you. Open yourself to others in your circle of friends and associates, and you may be surprised at who comes forward and says, "Yes, I understand, because that happened to me." Those words just might be the beginning of real comfort, practical assistance, and a lifelong friendship.

In difficult times, you might want to pull inside yourself, but that's not where you will find the solace that others can give you. Extend your hand and receive the comfort that one sensitive, caring, and been-there person can bring.

*It's another way to look at it!*

# Quotable...

Life has no blessing like a prudent friend.
*Euripides*

My friends are my estate.
*Emily Dickinson*

A friend is a gift you give yourself.
*Robert Louis Stevenson*

Our chief want in life is somebody who can make us do what we can. This is the service of a friend.
*Ralph Waldo Emerson*

Friendship is a sheltering tree.
*Samuel Taylor Coleridge*

Friendship that flows from the heart cannot be frozen by adversity, as the water that flows from the spring cannot congeal in winter.
*James Fenimore Cooper*

# The comfort of a friend…

… lets you know that you are not alone, for there's no place you can go that someone else has not been before.

… strengthens the ties of friendship, for you have discovered that this friend is there for you not only during fun and carefree times, but during sad times, too.

… opens new friendships, for the unexpected person who reaches out to comfort you could be the one who understands you, who cares about you, and loves you just because you're you.

… lightens your sorrows, for burdens shared are easier to carry, and difficult roads are best traveled with someone to walk beside you.

… allows the two of you to grow in appreciation of one another, for you never before realized how much it means to have a friend you can count on, share with, and love.

# A real friend helps us think our best thoughts…

A friend is never known until there is a burden to bear.

There is no physician like a true friend.

A friend is one who knows you as you are,
understands where you've been, accepts who
you've become, and still gently invites you to grow.

No route is long with good company.

In times of difficulty, friendship is put to the test.

Do not protect yourself by a fence, but rather by your
friends.

The smartest thing I ever said was, "Help me."

# …do our noblest deeds, be our finest selves.

# From *A Life for a Life*

*Oh, the comfort—*
*the inexpressible comfort*
*of feeling safe with a person—*
*having neither to weigh thoughts*
*nor measure words,*
*but pouring them all right out,*
*just as they are,*
*chaff and grain together;*
*certain that a faithful hand*
*will take and sift them,*
*keep what is worth keeping,*
*and then with the breath of kindness*
*blow the rest away.*

Dinah Maria Mulock Craik

# BROADENING YOUR BOUNDRIES

Why step outside the box
when you can charge outside the box?

# At various stages in life…

*…we find ourselves in a nice, comfortable place.*
We've accomplished things we're proud of…we enjoy
a circle of caring, supportive friends…we take pleasure
in the world around us. All this means we've grown,
because nothing but a certain amount of growth will
bring us to this point.

There's no one place in life, however, where we
can say, "That's it! I've seen all I want to see, done all
I want to do, felt all I want to feel." While we might
bask in satisfaction for a time, eventually we'll become
weary, bored with ourselves and the place in life that
seemed so fulfilling in the past. Continual growth,
ongoing experience, is essential to happiness.

At various times, you may need to rest—to stop
reaching out for a spell so you can renew your ener-
gies, review your priorities, and see where the next
places are that you'd like go, the new things you'd like
to learn, the fresh experiences you'd like to have. Then
it's time to broaden your boundaries!

A nice, comfortable place in life is the best place to
start deepening, widening, and expanding your love of
life—so go see what's out there, okay?

*It's another way to look at it!*

*Open yourself* to learning more about those things that interest you…exploring further the topics that grab your attention…understanding better the needs of those around you…letting your curiosity lead you in new directions.

*Refuse* to keep the status quo simply because it's comfortable and familiar…to settle for less than you are capable of doing…to believe you've reached a point where you can't do any better…to think there's no one who can teach you something new.

*Think big, think tall, think wide*…think long and hard about what you want to get out of life and, even more important, what you're willing to put into it…think less about your limitations and more about your possibilities…think of all that's out there for you.

*Stay involved with life*…let its sights, sounds, colors, wonders, and attractions keep you interested and engaged…try what you've never had the courage to try before…attempt something that others say you can't do…be daring…be different…take a chance.

*Create new opportunities* for tomorrow by taking opportunities that are available today...don't be afraid to change, because it's only through change that you can go forward, learn more, experience more, and be more.

*Live more!* Love life more deeply...appreciate your friends more intensely...listen more attentively...think more whimsically...respond more graciously...step more lightly...experience the world more profoundly.

*Surprise yourself* by discovering what you're capable of...by unearthing hidden talents...by realizing your true strengths...by getting to know how special you are...by living your principles and ideals...by enjoying your every day.

# If it is to be...

One who wants to know is better than one who already knows.

When you blame others, you give up your power to change.

Some pursue happiness—others create it.

If there is no wind, row.

You have to take it as it happens, but you should try to make it happen the way you want to take it.

You cannot discover new horizons unless you have the courage to lose sight of the shore.

## ...it's up to me.

# Quotable…

Dream lofty dreams, and as you dream, so shall you become. Your vision is the promise of what you shall at last unveil.
*John Ruskin*

If your daily life seems poor, do not blame it; blame yourself; tell yourself that you are not poet enough to call forth its riches.
*Rainer Maria Rilke*

I want, by understanding myself, to understand others. I want to be all that I am capable of becoming.
*Katherine Mansfield*

Things alter for the worse spontaneously, if they be not altered for the better designedly.
*Francis Bacon*

Destiny is not a matter of chance, it is a matter of choice; it is not a thing to be waited for, it is a thing to be achieved.
*William Jennings Bryan*

# FINDING COURAGE

Any chance you'll just step aside?

# Most of us will never face a giant on the battlefield…

*…but all of us are called upon* to face the giant inside us—fear. When we give in to fear, we're easily overrun by feelings of hopelessness and inadequacy. Opportunities we're afraid to take pass us by, and dreams we once cherished lie shattered beyond recovery. When fear gets the victory, we're left with a dim shadow of the life we had planned and hoped for. It doesn't have to happen again.

It takes courage to stand up for what you believe… go out on a limb with controversial ideas and opinions…compete for first place while everyone watches…make bold, decisive moves when the way ahead is far from clear. When you're living courageously, you hold yourself accountable for your words and actions… face difficult situations squarely and honestly…accept your situation and fulfill your obligations, even though there is hardship in store for you.

Though fear is never far from the daring heart, courage chops fear down to size. In addition, there's this truth about courage—every time you choose courage instead of fear, you gain even more courage for next time! Fear's shadow grows smaller and smaller…and smaller. That's when you realize you're a truly courageous person!

*It's another way to look at it!*

# Quotable...

Courage is resistance to fear, mastery of fear,
not absence of fear.
*Mark Twain*

Courage consists not in hazarding without fear,
but being resolutely minded in a just cause.
*Plutarch*

Dare and the world always yields; or if it beats you
sometimes, dare again, and it will succumb.
*William Makepeace Thackeray*

To have courage for whatever comes in life—
everything lies in that.
*Teresa of Avila*

To persevere, trusting in what hopes one has,
is courage. The coward despairs.
*Euripides*

Courage is the greatest of all the virtues. Because if
you haven't courage, you may not have an opportunity
to use any of the others.
*Samuel Johnson*

# A little lift of laughter…

*Courage!*

Dad and his young son were out on the lake fishing together when his son quietly said, "Dad, why are we here?" Dad steeled himself for a serious discussion of religion, purpose, ethics, and self-worth. "It's time," he thought, as he launched on a long, thoughtful, and heartfelt conversation. At its conclusion, Dad asked, "Does that answer your question, Son?"

"Not really, Dad," his son replied.

"No?" his dad said.

"What I meant was, why are we here when Mom asked us to pick her up from the store forty minutes ago?"

*Dare to Ride*

A biker riding a shiny new motorcycle on the highway pulled next to a car and knocked on the window. "Hey," he yelled to the driver, "ever driven a motorcycle?"

"No," replied the driver, and sped away.

The biker continued on until he saw another car, pulled up to it, and knocked on the window. "Say buddy," he shouted, "ever driven a motorcycle?"

"No, I haven't," the driver said, and sped away.

Then suddenly a curve appeared, and the cyclist flipped off his cycle and landed in a ditch by the side of the road. A Good Samaritan stopped and ran to his aid.

"Ever driven a motorcycle?" the biker asked his rescuer.

"Yes, certainly," the man replied, "driven one for thirty years."

"Tell me then," the man said, "where are the brakes?"

# …to help along the way!

# Courage is what it takes to stand up and speak…

Courage is fear that has said its prayers.

Nothing ventured, nothing gained.

Whatever you try to avoid stays until you confront it.

Courage is the right disposition toward fear.

The bravest way out of a problem is through it.

Boldness is nobleness of the mind.

A bold heart is half the battle won.

## …courage is also what it takes to sit down and listen.

# Live courageously!
# Say "Yes!" to…

… what you most cherish, like your dreams and goals, your values and principles. Are you going to let fear hold you back from these things?

… rational, objective thinking. Reject fantastical scenarios of disaster and vivid pictures of unlikely outcomes.

… acting in your best interests. If it will further your plans, benefit your future, or fulfill a good desire, do it!

… asking those who can provide information, help, support, or insight. Your questions might ruffle a few feathers, but they will open communication, increase awareness, and quell rumors and misunderstanding.

… making up your own mind and acting according to your own best interests and for the well-being of those dependent on you. Only you know, and some times it takes utmost courage to do what you know you need to do.

# LIVING WELL

Live big—that's my advice!

# Life has been given to you…

*…so what are you doing with it?* Those who treat life (and themselves) well aren't content to wander aimlessly through their days and years. Though in the course of life they must accept certain realities—not all of them pleasant—they make decisions likely to provide physical and emotional stability, healthy relationships, and fulfilling occupation.

Does life always work out as planned? No, because the gift of life comes without guarantees, yet with abundant possibilities. You have been given your life without an imposed blueprint, but with the liberty to explore many paths and choose for yourself the best. Though there are "musts" for a sane and rational life, you have more ways to express yourself than you may think. There are limits, but the limits are often much further away than you may imagine.

Life enables you to create order, find purpose, extend kindness, and experience joy. These things don't come naturally! Each one takes a down-to-earth assessment of your abilities and your situation, along with a willingness to learn new ways of responding if the old ways aren't working for you. Where there's a gap between where you are now and where you'd like to be, it's within your power to set realistic goals, make actionable plans, and take responsibility for God's great gift to you—your life.

*It's another way to look at it!*

# A life well-lived...

*We are always getting ready to live, but never living.*
Ralph Waldo Emerson

*Take pleasure in everyday wonders.* Though you have hopes and plans for tomorrow, today—these hours, this moment—is what you have been given. You may not be where you hope to go yet, but for a life well-lived, savor each step along the way.

*To get the full value of joy,*
*you must have someone to divide it with.*
Mark Twain

*Stay close to friends and family.* Though all relationships take work to develop, nurture, repair, and maintain, it's work that yields rewards found nowhere else. Only through strong relationships can you grow and help others grow; on with and among others will you know true joy.

*Living well and beautifully and justly are all one thing.*
Socrates

*Act with fairness, respect, kindness.* Strong values and positive principles to live by confer self-worth and open your eyes to the worth of others. When you know yourself as one beloved of God, you realize others are His children, too.

*It is in his pleasure that a man really lives.*
Agnes Repplier

*Pursue personal interests.* You were given a unique
set of talents, abilities, and interests meant to bring
you joy and satisfaction in life. It might happen that
through following your own seemingly cockamamie
dream, you not only enrich your life, but the lives of
others, too.

*Laugh and the world laughs with you.*
Ella Wheeler Wilcox

*Cultivate a light heart.* Though sorrow, hardship, and
seriousness are part of life, each is eased with kindly
humor, gentle understanding, and the warmth of a
caring smile. Allow yourself to laugh today, and you
have lived well today!

*The purpose of life is to live it,*
*to taste experience to the utmost,*
*to reach out eagerly and without fear*
*for newer and richer experience.*
Eleanor Roosevelt

*Possess purpose.* Unless you have a sense of what you
want your life to mean, to stand for, and to accomplish, you'll remain aimless. Specific objectives determine your current path, while your guiding beliefs and
values define your life's direction.

# You are younger today than you ever will be again…

Life wants to give you the best,
but you must work for it.

Nature has given you the power or the desire
to do this, to another that. Each bird must sing
with his own throat.

Bloom where you are planted.

Words are mere bubbles of water,
but deeds are drops of gold.

More powerful than the will to live well is
the courage to begin.

It isn't our position, but our disposition that
makes us happy.

## …make use of it for the sake of tomorrow.

# Quotable...

It is impossible to live pleasurably without living wisely, well and justly; and impossible to live wisely, well and justly without living pleasurably.
*Epicurus*

The life which is unexamined is not worth living.
*Plato*

Life is not first lived and then understood;
it is poorly lived till understood.
*George A. Gordon*

Man is fond of counting his troubles, but he does not count his joys. If he counted them up as he ought to, he would see that every lot has enough happiness provided for it.
*Fyodor Dostoevsky*

People are always good company when they are doing what they really enjoy.
*Samuel Butler*

Live all you can; it's a mistake not to. It doesn't so much matter what you do in particular, so long as you have your life. If you haven't had that, what have you had?
*Henry James*

# LOVING THE MOMENT

Sometimes everything's
downright perfect!

# If you have ever watched puppies or kittens at play…

*…you've seen spontaneous joy in action!* The little bundles of fur are completely immersed in fun and pleasure, and they're not about to miss a single moment.

How often do you allow yourself to experience spontaneous joy? Inside you, underneath layers of learned reserve, guarded responses, and measured moves, there lies a will to live lightly, freely, and joyfully. Yet, if you're like most of us, you're waiting for the perfect circumstances and the perfect time to seize joy. Meanwhile…

Meanwhile, joy waits for you right where you are—in the muddled, messy, imperfect here and now. Joy doesn't need a specific situation or wonderful circumstances, but only your delight in the warmth of the sun on your face and the sound of rain on your roof…the voice of your best friend and the taste of your favorite dessert…the privilege of doing the task at hand and the satisfaction of a job well done.

Every moment of giving to others because of love… stepping out to follow a dream…pausing along the way to admire a flower…loving the day simply because it's here is a moment brimming with heart-lifting, smile-bringing, blessing-giving joy!

*It's another way to look at it!*

*Live attentively!*
There is nothing more valuable than today—this hour, this moment. Notice it, embrace it, and engage it with genuine enthusiasm. Give it all you've got!

*Live abundantly!*
Expect more out of life than routine. Within you, there are blessings to be discovered, possibilities to be imagined, and opportunities to explore. But like a piece of fruit on a tree, you need to reach out and take it before you can enjoy the fullness of its flavor.

*Live spontaneously!*
With kindness and love in your heart, you can trust yourself to respond from the heart, freely and naturally. You can let go, because where goodness is, goodness emerges. Don't be afraid to express yourself.

*Live joyfully!*
Make up your mind to smile, laugh, and enjoy what's around you. Compliment people, admire nature, and give yourself a pat on the back. Even if things aren't great right now, a joyful attitude will make them look much better.

# Quotable...

Gladly accept the gifts of the present hour.
*Horace*

Know the true value of time; snatch, seize, and enjoy
every moment of it.
*Lord Chesterfield*

May you live all the days of your life.
*Jonathan Swift*

Time lost is time when we have not lived a full human
life, time unenriched by experience, creative endeavor,
enjoyment, and suffering.
*Dietrich Bonhoeffer*

Each day provides its own gifts.
*Martial*

That man is happiest who lives from day to day and
asks no more, garnering the simple goodness of life.
*Euripides*

Much may be done in those little shreds and patches of
time which every day produces, and which most men
throw away.
*Charles Caleb Colton*

# A little life of laughter...

*Simple Pleasures*
" I take pleasure in the simple things in life," a woman confided to her friend, "like seeing the guy who sped past me on the highway pulled over by the police at the next exit."

*Timely Question*
How do you explain counterclockwise to someone with a digital watch?

*When?*
Having dated her boyfriend for quite some time with no discussion of marriage, a young woman decided she should drop some hints. That evening, they went to a Chinese restaurant, and her boyfriend asked, "How do you like your rice, steamed or fried?"
She smiled and said, "Thrown."

*Why Dogs Have It So Good*
They're super-excited to see the same people every day. They can get a whole afternoon's entertainment out of a single rawhide bone.
They can plop down and snooze in a roomful of people, and no one takes offense.
They don't have to worry about bathing every day.
They can drool without embarrassment.
Everything they eat tastes like a gourmet meal.
Puppy love lasts a whole life long!

# With every rising of the sun...

The most important thing in our lives is what we are doing now.

Time stays long enough for anyone who will use it.

The morning has gold in its mouth.

Time is so precious that God gives it only moment by moment.

A day is a span of time no one is wealthy enough to waste.

You can't make footprints in the sands of time while sitting down.

## ...think of your life as just begun.

# ENJOYING THE JOURNEY

Life is a mooooving experience!

# You know about goals and milestones...

*...but more important than reaching them* is enjoying the journey it takes to get there. Any long-term aim, any worthwhile aspiration, requires effort, dedication, commitment, and time. It's going to take up perhaps years, if not decades, of your life; so it only makes sense to keep the goal in front of you, but your mind and attention, your head and your heart, focused on the day.

Even if you're struggling with a situation or challenge that isn't particularly to your liking, there's still an immense amount of daily learning and inner strengthening going on. You don't want to miss or overlook any of it! Though you hope for a speedy finish to the whole business, everything that happens in your life offers the chance to live more fully, act more wisely, and love more deeply.

Every day of your life is the real thing—an opportunity to move forward with grace and dignity, to mine the hours for moments of joy and heartwarming humor, to heighten your appreciation of yourself, the people around you, and all creation.

Goals are great, but they're in the future. Far greater—and far more exciting—is the journey it takes to get there!

*It's another way to look at it!*

# Enjoy the journey…

*… by noticing those little moments* that flutter by so
quickly, like the play of sun through the trees, the
song of a bird in the branches, the fragrance of
springtime flowers in the air.

*… by appreciating the sacred side* of an ordinary day;
like the love behind a home cooked meal, the caring
beneath a kindly act, the generosity that comes when
ever someone says: "I'm always here for you."

*…by cherishing the companionship* of those you love,
like the encouraging words of a caring friend, the
understanding smile that lights the face you love to
see, the sound of someone far away whose voice
brings back the best of memories.

*… by nurturing your spirit in positive ways,* like spending
time in quiet reflection and attentive prayer, gaining
insight and guidance through time-honored truths,
acting in accordance with your highest ideals.

*... by facing your challenges,* like owning up to your weaknesses and shortcomings, and making changes for the better; identifying your limitations, and seeking help and support to overcome them; admitting your worries and fears, and handing them over to God.

*... by opening yourself to a higher purpose,* like committing yourself to excellence in everything you do and say; choosing challenging and worthwhile goals; standing up for, and working for, dignity, justice, and respect for all.

*... by dedicating yourself to positive habits,* like maintaining an optimistic outlook; shunning excess, greed, and passing gratification; refusing to see yourself, or allow others to describe you, as a victim; looking for the lightness, the balm of laughter, in every situation.

*... by delighting in being you,* because there's no one like you—never was, and never will be. Today and every day, enjoy the privilege of being on the journey— your journey!

# Quotable...

Not I, nor anyone else, can travel that road for you. You must travel it by yourself.
*Walt Whitman*

True progress quietly and persistently moves along without notice.
*Francis de Sales*

The real voyage of discovery consists not in seeking new landscapes, but in having new eyes.
*Marcel Proust*

To travel hopefully is a better thing than to arrive, and the true success is to labor.
*Robert Louis Stevenson*

Happiness is not a state to arrive at,
but a manner of traveling.

*Magaret Lee Runbeck*

*There's always another way
to look at it!*